W9-AHF-355

how to start a home-based
Craft Business

how to start a home-based

Craft Business

Sixth Edition

Kenn Oberrecht and Patrice Lewis

gpp®

Guilford, Connecticut

Flagstaff Public Library
Flagstaff, Arizona

To buy books in quantity for corporate use
or incentives, call **(800) 962-0973**
or e-mail **premiums@GlobePequot.com**.

Copyright © 1994, 1997, 2000, 2004, 2007, 2011 Morris Book Publishing, LLC
Sixth Edition Printing 2011

ALL RIGHTS RESERVED. No part of this book may be reproduced or transmitted in any form by
any means, electronic or mechanical, including photocopying and recording, or by any information storage and retrieval system, except as may be expressly permitted in writing from the
publisher. Requests for permission should be addressed to Globe Pequot Press, Attn: Rights and
Permissions Department, P.O. Box 480, Guilford, CT 06437.

Editorial Director: Cynthia Hughes
Editor: Katie Benoit
Project Editor: Tracee Williams
Text Design: Sheryl P. Kober
Layout: Kevin Mak

ISSN: 1548-671X
ISBN: 978-0-7627-6363-4

Printed in the United States of America
10 9 8 7 6 5 4 3 2 1

This book's purpose is to provide accurate and authoritative information on the topics covered.
It is sold with the understanding that neither the authors nor the publisher is engaged in rendering legal, financial, accounting, and other professional services. Neither Globe Pequot Press
nor the authors assumes any liability resulting from action taken based on the information
included herein. Mention of a company name does not constitute endorsement.

Flagstaff Public Library
Flagstaff, Arizona

For my very good friend Peggy Patton

Contents

Introduction

Have we met? I feel as if I know you. Let me see if I have it right. You're a creative person, and you like working with your hands. You enjoy crafts as a hobby and have gotten pretty good at what you do. Many of your friends and relatives proudly display the craft items you have given them at Christmas, for birthdays, and on other gift-giving occasions.

Maybe you've won some ribbons at the county fair or at some local craft club exhibits. You've gained confidence in yourself and in your craft. People have told you time and again that you should be selling what you make, and you've begun to believe them. After all, you've seen far worse on sale at gift shops, galleries, and craft fairs. You wonder how a person might go about getting into the business. The idea's a little scary, but it's exciting too.

Plus, with economic times so tight, perhaps you're thinking about how you can earn some extra money doing the things you're already doing.

Or maybe you have even bigger dreams. Wouldn't it be great to chuck the nine-to-five, be your own boss, and run your own business your way? No more long, boring, and costly commutes. No more workplace hassles and politics. You'll start pocketing the profits instead of making profits for others. You'll be closer to home and family. You'll be your own boss, and your successes will be based on your own skills and enthusiasm. And you can take a day off now and then simply because you want to. It's possible, isn't it?

Of course it's possible. It's even probable, if you put your mind to it, research the prospects, develop a sound plan, and stay on course. What's more, it won't cost as much as you might think.

You no doubt already own some of the necessary equipment and can afford to buy the required materials. You possess important knowledge and experience in at least one craft, or you're willing to learn. Best of all, as a home-based entrepreneur, you won't have to borrow a bundle to pay the lease on a shop downtown or at the mall.

In most ways, starting and running your own home-based craft business is probably easier than you think; in a few ways, it might be a little tougher, but there are no obstacles impossible to surmount. You already possess the initiative and inventiveness to create something out of virtually nothing. Armed with a little extra knowledge on how to run the business side of things, you have the potential to build an enterprise that can supplement or even supplant your current income. What a wonderful feeling!

In the pages that follow, you'll find a wealth of valuable business information and many helpful tips and tricks that will take the edge off that little pang of fear and give you the courage to take the big step.

So this is a book for artisans, but it's not about any specific craft. Rather, it covers the craft *business* and tells you what you need to know about operating such a business from your home. In the following chapters, you'll find practical solutions to problems and plenty of solid advice on how to tap your creative skills to earn a living.

If you haven't inherited millions or won the lottery, you're going to have to work for a living for the rest of your life. Why not make a career of doing what you most enjoy? It won't just happen, but you can make it happen.

This book will help you along your path. So read, heed, and apply—and join the thousands of successful crafters, artists, and entrepreneurs who have left behind the nine-to-five drudgery and become home-based craft business stars.

01 Starting Your Home-Based Craft Business

Among the many businesses that can be operated from a home, craft businesses are particularly suitable. Most craft objects are relatively small and easy to store and transport. The tools are easy to use at home and won't disturb your neighbors. Manufacturing materials aren't gravely hazardous and probably won't pose any major storage problems.

Craft professionals shouldn't find working at home any more difficult than craft hobbyists do. Depending on your craft, the transition from hobbyist to professional requires little or no adjustment in the way you manufacture your products. You may already have sufficient work space in the form of a shop or workroom. Because you will be increasing production volume, you will probably have to find or create adequate storage space, and you'll want an office of some sort for attending to all the details of running a business.

For many would-be artisan entrepreneurs, it's difficult to muster the necessary confidence to approach the marketplace. Confidence is every bit as important as skill in your chosen craft. You must have confidence in your craft, in yourself, and in your ability to run a business and sell your products.

Don't think of your products as homemade, but rather as meticulously handcrafted to exacting standards. Handcrafted products are in great demand, because they provide customers with an elusive quality too infrequently encountered these days: good old Yankee craftsmanship. Carefully handcrafted products are better made than assembly-line stampouts and cheap foreign imports and are unique because of their quality.

Look Before You Leap

Before getting down to the business of business, you have some pleasant preliminary work ahead of you. Visit the kinds of shops, galleries, and stores in which you would like to see your products sold. Browse, observe the customers, talk to the proprietors, and ask for advice.

Attend local and nearby arts-and-crafts shows, Christmas bazaars, sidewalk exhibits, wine festivals, food fairs, and other events where there are craft booths and displays. Look for ideas and take notes. Watch the customers to see what stops them and what entices them to buy. Talk to the exhibitors when they're not busy. Ask them about their experiences and tell them of your plans. Seek the advice of these readily available experts.

Don't trust your memory. Take notes, and later review them carefully. You'll be surprised how the ideas you find will breed others. Jot them down too. All this will become a solid foundation upon which to build a secure business.

Should You Start Your Own Business?

No one but you can determine whether or not you should start your own craft business, but certain indicators can lead you toward the right choice. Of course, if you have little or no skill in any craft, minimal manual dexterity, and no interest in getting better, you needn't go any further; find yourself another business. If, on the other hand, you're a competent artisan—even a good one—but have no patience for or interest in managing a business, then you'd better work for someone else for the rest of your career and treat crafts as a hobby.

Even if the notion of being self-employed as a home-based artisan appeals to you, and you either now possess or are willing to attain the necessary skills and knowledge, you still must question yourself thoroughly to learn where your strengths and weaknesses lie. This is part of the planning stage of your business: a process that's never too early to start and one that should continue throughout the life of your business.

Below are ten questions you need to answer in as much detail as possible before you start your business. So sit down with a pen and a pad of paper, and answer as many of them as you can. You probably won't be able to respond to all the questions in one sitting. Those left unanswered will guide you toward your weaknesses or the areas where you simply need to do some work or research, or perhaps seek help.

Answer the questions as completely and honestly as possible; to do less is to fool yourself and court disaster.

1. *Why do you want to start a home-based craft business?* Provide as many reasons as you can, such as being your own boss, having an opportunity to spend more time with your family, gaining control of your career, getting out of a dead-end job, avoiding the hassles of commuting, and anything else you can think of.

2. *What craft experience and management skills can you bring to your new business?* List craft-related jobs and management positions you've held, courses you've taken, books you've read, and how they have helped to prepare you. If you identify weaknesses in either area, explain how you plan to overcome them. If you've never held a management position, perhaps your plan to gain the necessary skills is to launch a research effort at your local library and bookstore, to take business courses at a local community college, to sign up for seminars offered by a small-business organization or cooperative, or a combination of these.

3. *How much space will you need for your new business?* First, determine what kind of space you will need: office, workshop, studio, warehouse or storage room, sales area or display room. Every home-based business must have an office. You'll need some kind of workroom, workshop, studio, or a combination of these. Nobody ever has enough storage space. Although some businesses might get by with no more than a large storage cabinet or closet, most craft businesses require more, some far more. After determining your space requirements, estimate the size in square feet. Sit down with paper, pencil, and ruler and lay out your work area. (There are computer programs that will help you do this.) Allow for furniture and equipment so that you'll get an idea of how much space this business is going to take up. (For more information, see chapter 2 under "Setting Up Your Business Space.")

4. *How do you plan to accommodate the space demands of your new business?* Will you temporarily set up a home office at one end of the dining-room table or put a desk in your bedroom and work there? There is nothing wrong with that; many home-based entrepreneurs start out this way. Will you set up a permanent office in an unused room? Can your office double as a studio or workroom, or do you need separate rooms? Do you have garage, basement, or attic space you can convert? Can you build on? Everyone will have different answers to these questions; renters are more restricted than owners, and persons who live in small dwellings are more restricted than

those who have plenty of space. For some, the answers might change within a short time. If you plan to move within the next five years, you would do well to list short-term and long-term space considerations. (Chapter 8, "Taxes and Record Keeping," covers the use of a home as a business.)

5. *What are your immediate and future equipment needs and how will you meet them?* List all arts-and-crafts equipment you will need to start and operate your business for one year. Depending on the nature of your craft(s), that could include a wide assortment of hand tools, power tools, and various specialized instruments. List all office and other equipment you will need for the same period: computer, telephones, calculator, filing cabinets, office furniture, vehicle. Similarly, list your projected equipment needs for the next five years. In each category, indicate equipment you already own and note how you expect to acquire what you don't have. Keep in mind that in addition to acquiring equipment, you'll probably need to update and upgrade some during your first five years of business. (See chapter 2 under "Setting Up Your Business Space.")

6. *What licenses, permits, and laws do you need to know about to operate a business from your home?* Laws vary from state to state, county to county, and city to city. Your state may require you to file your business name with a state agency or to apply for a business or vendor's license. You might have to obtain a permit from your county government. There could be city ordinances regulating the operation of home businesses, even from one neighborhood to the next. You need to know about all such obstacles and determine how you'll overcome them before you go into business. (Chapter 6, "The Legal Aspects of Your Craft Business," offers more information on zoning ordinances, licenses, and permits.)

7. *How much cash will you need to run your business for one year and where will it come from?* This is no place to fudge the figures. Be as honest and as accurate as possible, even though you're making an estimate, and possibly not a very educated one at that. Remember, if you must err on money matters, it's always best to err on the side of fiscal conservatism: Overestimate the payables and underestimate the receivables—any outcome to the contrary will be a pleasant surprise. Estimate what it will cost you to run the business for a year, and don't forget to include your own salary as part of the cost. Now determine where the operating capital will come from: savings, spouse's

income, pension or retirement income, the business itself, or elsewhere. (For more information on financial planning, see chapters 4, 5 and 7.)

8. *Who are your competitors, how are they doing, and how do you expect to overtake them in the marketplace?* The way you deal with this question depends on the kinds of craftwork you plan to engage in and how many other local artisans work in the same area. If certain kinds of crafts are popular in your community or region, and you plan to work with those same crafts, you'll be in competition with many other local artisans. If they're all driving fancy vehicles and living in expensive houses, there's obviously plenty of room for competition. If they're barely scratching out an existence, however, that could mean the supply is outstripping the demand, and you might need to look for another niche. Chances are, reality lies somewhere between the two extremes. If you have a particular area of expertise—say, clock making, picture framing, or basket weaving—in a small community, you could be the only artisan so skilled and may well fill a niche. Spend some time with this question, and answer it carefully. This is your first step into the realm of market analysis. (You'll find more marketing information and ideas in chapter 3, "Marketing Your Craft Business.")

9. *What are your short-term financial and personal goals for your new business? In other words, what do you expect to earn and accomplish during your first year of operation?* This question relates to question 1 and goes beyond question 7. Here you need to focus, get more specific. You should lay out objectives that go beyond mere subsistence or "just getting by." What are your goals? What do you expect your income to be by the end of your first year? Will you have others working for you? What sort of hourly or daily rates or commission fees will you be demanding by then? How will you have improved or branched out? What will you have learned?

10. *What are your long-term financial and personal goals?* Now discuss everything you covered in question 9 in terms of a five-year plan. How big do you expect your business to be in five years? How skilled an artisan do you hope to be? What sort of customers do you expect to have by then? Will your business continue to grow, or will you want it to level off at some point? Do you plan to hire help? Will you branch out into other crafts, arts, and allied fields? Will you get rich?

Market Survey—Retail Outlet Sample

Business _____   Contact Date_____

Street _____   Contact_____

Suite _____ P.O. Box_____   Title_____

City_____   Phone (_____) _____

State _____ Zip _____   Phone (_____) _____

Weekday Hours_____   Fax (_____)_____

Saturday Hours_____   E-mail_____

Sunday Hours_____   Days Closed_____

_____ Gallery   _____ Gift Shop   _____ Department Store   _____ General Store

_____ Craft Shop   _____ Craft Mall   _____ Antiques Shop   _____ Antiques Mall

_____ Toy Store   _____ Other _____

Description of Merchandise _____

_____

_____

Best-Selling Items_____

_____

_____

Visit/Interview Notes & Comments_____

_____

_____

_____

_____

Business _The Country Mercantile_   Contact Date _May 23, 2011_

Street _1615 River Road_   Contact _Lily Putian_

Suite _____ P.O. Box _1851_   Title _Owner_

City _Connorsville_   Phone (_800_) _555-5432_

State _Indiana_ Zip _47331_   Phone (_123_) _555-9876_

Weekday Hours _10:00 a.m. to 6:00 p.m._   Fax (_123_) _555-9898_

Saturday Hours _9:00 a.m. to 6:00 p.m._   E-mail _LilyPut@Indiana.store.net_

Sunday Hours _Noon to 5:00 p.m._   Days Closed _Monday_

_X_ Gallery   ____ Gift Shop   ____ Department Store   ____ General Store

____ Craft Shop   ____ Craft Mall   ____ Antiques Shop   ____ Antiques Mall

____ Toy Store   ____ Other _____

Description of Merchandise _Clothing, boots, specialty and gourmet foods, cookware,_
cutlery, kitchen utensils, small appliances, canning equipment and supplies, mugs,
glasses, wine, microbrews, books.

Best-Selling Items _Anything for the kitchen and cooking._

Visit/Interview Notes & Comments _Lily is interested in carrying alder mug trees,_
laminated cutlery blocks, hardwood herb & spice jars, and maple cutting
boards. Will be buying stock in July; I should phone or send order sheet.
She wants ONE GIANT MUG TREE IMMEDIATELY. Agreed to deliver
by June 15.

Hobby versus Business

Just as there are amateur athletes who are as skilled as or better than their professional counterparts, many serious amateur artists and artisans are every bit as good as most of the people who make a living in their field. The difference has less to do with proficiency than what people choose to do with it.

The distinction used to be a simple one: Amateurs don't get paid for their work; professionals do. That line has been blurred considerably in recent years. While many amateurs are satisfied to treat crafts as a hobby—creating objects for their own enjoyment and perhaps entering amateur competitions to win ribbons and the occasional plum prize—some sell their work to help defray costs. Whether it's a hobby, an avocation, or a profession, a craft can be expensive. Most materials are costly, and the equipment sometimes outrageously so. As a hobbyist, you might be able to offset some of your expenses by selling your work. As a professional, you'd better be able to sell enough to pay all your expenses and make a decent profit as well.

One of the most attractive aspects of craftwork is the possibility of advancing from hobby to career, a sequence practitioners of other professions seldom enjoy. We don't see amateur contractors, for example, building houses and office complexes for the joy of it, or hobby surgeons doing coronary bypasses evenings and weekends in their spare time. Many artisans, however, work first for the fun of it, then study and master enough techniques to advance to the level of serious amateur, and ultimately put that knowledge and experience to work earning money.

Part-Time versus Full-Time

The artisan who decides to work as a home-based professional is faced with deciding between part-time and full-time work. I suspect most of us begin working part-time and gradually or eventually steer our businesses into full-time operation. Starting part-time offers many advantages, and I recommend you seriously consider this route. Here are some of the things you can do when starting out part-time:

- Work at home in your spare time while retaining a full-time job and its steady income.
- Run a part-time home-based craft business and work at another part-time job to make ends meet.
- Retain the benefits package your employer offers while establishing your home-based business.

- Gain professional experience that will prove invaluable when you go full-time.
- Set up adequate business facilities in your spare time without financial hardship.
- Gradually invest in craft and office equipment and furniture.
- See to numerous details at your leisure, such as a logo, business cards, letterhead, brochures, a Yellow Pages listing, and an online platform.
- Set up files and establish customer accounts, vendor accounts, and bank accounts.
- Build an excellent credit rating and a solid professional reputation.
- Let your business grow until it's making your projected or required full-time income.
- Build a cash reserve that's big enough to finance your first year's full-time operation.
- Get a feel for the potential of your business and markets before making a major commitment.

You can do all this and more as a part-time home-based artisan and entrepreneur. You might continue working part-time indefinitely, until you feel like going into full-time business. Or you can do as I did: continue stowing away cash from the income of your part-time business while gaining valuable experience in other related fields.

I ran my home-based business part-time for nearly four years, enjoying the diversity of the various kinds of work I was involved in while gaining a tremendous amount of experience. By the time I was ready to work full-time at it, I was making regular sales and earning a fairly steady income. I had established many contacts, set up good working facilities in my home, acquired the equipment I needed, and built good working files and a reference library. I had also established all the necessary accounts with vendors, banks, and oil and credit card companies.

Four years as a part-time entrepreneur also enabled me to experiment with a great array of equipment and to gradually acquire more and upgrade what I had. I plowed my first year's part-time income back into the business to upgrade existing equipment. The following year I started investing in new equipment and putting aside some profits to build a cash reserve.

By the time I was ready for my home-based business to become a full-time occupation, all of my equipment was new, nearly new, or in excellent condition, which assured me of good service with minimal downtime.

I bought a new IBM typewriter and a few other office items, as well as several new tools and six months' worth of office supplies and materials. I paid for everything from the business cash reserve I had accumulated in four years of part-time work and had enough left to cover my first year's expenses and salary. I can't think of a safer, more comfortable way to start a full-time, home-based business.

Of course, there is a downside to starting and running a part-time home-based business while trying to hold down a full-time job elsewhere. It's difficult to do justice to your business while giving your best efforts to an employer. Your first loyalties must go to that employer, which is often a stretch and a hectic way to live and work. But it's also excellent training and might be the only feasible way to realize your dream.

Learning Your Craft

I assume that most people who plan to start and operate a home-based craft business already possess some craft skills. At the very least, you should have some grasp of the basic tools and techniques of your chosen craft(s) and an abiding interest in learning as much as possible about every aspect of the business.

Taking Courses

My first recommendation is to take courses from good teachers at a local college, technical school, or arts-and-crafts school. I stress: *good teachers*. The same course can be taught by two different teachers, and the two can be as similar as platinum and pig iron.

Your first job is to find a course. Then you need to determine the quality and competence of the teacher. You can't be shy. Phone or visit the teacher and ask for a summary of what the course will cover. Tell the teacher what you need and expect from the course, and ask if this course will fulfill those requirements. Find out what texts are to be used and review them. Talk to the teacher's former students. You should be able to tell within one or two class meetings whether you've found a guru or a bozo. In case of the latter, drop the course, get your money back, lodge a complaint with the school, and look elsewhere for instruction.

Again, don't be afraid to ask questions, and don't think you'll appear stupid for doing so. As someone who has taught a variety of college courses and workshops that range from basic to graduate level, I can tell you that one of a teacher's greatest rewards is being able to work with inquisitive and interested students—people who are there to learn.

Learning by Reading

Another way to learn is by reading, and even small public libraries generally have dozens of craft titles on their shelves. In the small town where I live, the public library has nearly 500 craft books listed in fifty-eight subject areas.

You probably already know about some of the general and specialized crafts magazines, but you would do well to spend time learning what other periodicals are available. You should subscribe to the best magazines in your field and plan to purchase the better how-to guides and reference manuals as a way of building a good business library.

In the absence of a good basic course, locally available, I recommend a series of trips to bookstores, public and college libraries, and magazine stands. Browse through the craft titles until you find books on crafts you're skilled or interested in. They should be clearly written and well illustrated. Make a list of all the relevant titles and begin investigating them. Quickly skim through the books to determine those that are worth borrowing from a library, those you'll want to purchase for your own library, and the poorly written and illustrated books that aren't worth your time and money.

Do the same with magazines. At a good public library and at local magazine stands, you'll find periodicals worth reading, some even worth subscribing to. At the library's reference section, check the *Readers' Guide to Periodical Literature* for titles in your interest areas.

As a crafts professional, you'll want to subscribe to *The Crafts Report* (www .craftsreport.com), a magazine that bills itself as "the business journal for the crafts industry." This monthly publication runs regular columns and departments, as well as feature articles on topics of interest and importance to craft professionals. It tracks nationwide trends, announces shows and fairs state by state, and puts readers in touch with peers and prospects. (See the "Source Directory" at the back of this book for more details.)

Don't forget business literature. Investigate the business book sections at local libraries and bookstores, and pay special attention to volumes prepared for home-based business managers. Do likewise in the computer book sections. Also review the various business and computer magazines that are available.

Internet access allows you to browse the virtual bookshelves at giant online bookstores, such as amazon.com and barnesandnoble.com. There you can make general subject searches for craft, business, and computer books. You can also search for specific titles, examine their tables of contents, and read chapter excerpts as well as publishers' and readers' reviews.

You can't conclude this initial research project and consider the job done. You'll have to continue reading books and magazines from now on, not only to learn what you don't yet know, but also to keep abreast of the ever-changing technology.

Workshops and Seminars

You should be able to find craft workshops and business seminars in your part of the country. You'll learn about these in national magazines and local newspapers, as well as through direct-mail advertising once your name and address get established on various mailing lists as those of the owner of a home-based craft business.

Other good sources for information about workshops and seminars are your local chamber of commerce, the business department of any nearby college or university, and your community's Small Business Development Center (SBDC).

The Optional Apprenticeship

Sometimes it's possible to learn from others as an apprentice of sorts. If you can stand the low pay (usually minimum wage) and gofer chores, working as an assistant to an established artisan can be a good way to learn a craft from an expert. Keep in mind, too, that although your paycheck is small, what you learn on the job might otherwise cost you dearly in the form of tuition paid to a school.

Artist versus Artisan

Are you an artist or an artisan? Or could you possibly be both? Often, a thin line separates the two categories; sometimes the line is invisible. That is, some artists are also skilled artisans, and a good many artisans are truly artistic in their endeavors. It's often difficult to distinguish artworks from craftworks.

For example, the watercolorist who learns how to mount, mat, and frame watercolors is an artist who engages in a craft to benefit the artwork. A good many artisans clearly have artistic abilities that enhance their craftworks and increase their value and salability.

Some people seem to have innate artistic abilities, but they are the exceptions. Most practicing artists have an aptitude for art but were not born with the skills they possess; they learned them. The same is true of artisans.

Both artists and artisans work with spatial relationships and must be conscious of size, shape, form, design, and composition in their respective works. Therefore, most artisans can profit from the study of art and design. Both fine and applied arts are disciplines you might consider studying as a way of improving your craft and making yourself a more versatile and skilled artisan.

Specialist versus Generalist

The decision to work as a specialist or generalist depends largely on acquired skills, personal choice, and the realities of the marketplace. Most artisans begin as specialists because their skills are limited. Those who decide to remain specialists usually do so because they enjoy working in one craft area and have found an eager market for their products.

There's certainly nothing wrong with the single-craft approach to the business, as long as you are happy with what you are doing and are generating the kind of income you need or want. Diversifying, however, is a good way to spread out your liabilities, reduce risks, and add other skills to your repertoire. For the person who is easily bored, diversity might be the only route to success in the home-based craft business.

Whether to specialize or generalize is mainly up to you. The only advice I will offer in this regard is to learn your craft well; then evaluate your circumstances in light of the marketplace. If you then wish to begin diversifying, learn your next crafts equally well, one at a time.

You also probably will do best to work in related or similar areas. This will enable you to use some of the tools and equipment required for one craft in other crafts. For example, if you're a woodworker, you'll probably find it relatively easy and inexpensive to move into picture framing or marquetry. The tools and materials you use for making wooden furnishings and fixtures will prove valuable if you start making wooden toys, puzzles, games, models, and decoys. Country, regional, and holiday crafts are other possibilities for the skilled woodworker.

Salable Crafts

For the most part, the home-based artisan can work in any craft area. Your options are manifold. You can pick the craft you're best at or most interested in and build a business around that. You can specialize or diversify depending on your skill. To compete as a specialist—say, in ceramics—you should set out to become the best ceramist in your community. If you decide to work in several or many handicrafts, you needn't strive to be, and probably won't be, the best in your community in each craft. You'll have to be good in each, though, and should strive to be outstanding. You might thereby prove yourself the most versatile artisan in your vicinity.

It's important that you have some idea of the direction you want your business to take, and, again, planning is crucial. You guessed it: It's time, once more, for the trusty pad and pen. List all the crafts you can think of. Identify those that interest you most. If you can, pick the one that's most exciting to you; if you can't, don't worry about it.

I was able to come up with a list of fifty popular American crafts, which I'm including here as a way of helping you create your own list. See if you can add to it. Then highlight those that appeal most to you.

By performing this simple exercise, you may have already identified the craft you are most suited for and might want to specialize in. On the other hand, you may have discovered that your interests are broad and that you are most inclined to be a diversified artisan.

You needn't set out immediately to specialize in anything, or to generalize, for that matter. You could find in a year or two that you're being pulled one way or another. It doesn't matter. As long as you continue to stay in touch with your own feelings and ambitions, as long as you continue to plan and set realistic goals, and as long as you continue to strive toward creative excellence, all that remains is to acquire business acumen.

Artisan Turned Manager

Being a self-employed artisan has its advantages and disadvantages. One important advantage is that you have the greatest possible amount of control over the business you're involved in when you're the one who's running it. The time and energy required to manage your business, however, are time and energy not devoted to the aspect we artisans enjoy most: the creative process.

A fact you must face at the outset, before you carry this idea of running your own business any further, is that as a self-employed artisan, you probably will spend considerably less time creating craft items than you will seeing to all the business management chores and paperwork. The best you can hope and plan for is that your work will be equally divided between the creative process and management. If you don't have a taste for management, get a job, or keep the one you have.

If you work for someone else, you need only be good at the job for which you were hired. As the owner/manager of a home-based craft business, however, you will not only have to demonstrate creative expertise, but you will also have to be a competent manager. In your own home-based business, you wear all the hats.

Popular American Crafts

Calligraphy	Doll making
Stained glass projects	Rug making
Tole painting	Macramé
Toy making	Knife making
Making puzzles	Making fishing tackle
Making games	Gunsmithing
Jewelry making	Folk art
Cloisonné enameling	Silversmithing
Leather craft	Making archery tackle
Ceramics	Coppersmithing
Pottery	Blacksmithing
Needlecraft	Tincrafting
Making decoys	Woodworking
Building clocks	Marquetry
Kitchen crafts	Wood carving
Basketry	Sign making
Picture framing	Country crafts
Textile crafts	Regional crafts
Candle making	Native crafts
Tile crafts	Holiday crafts
Block printing	Garden crafts
Silk-screening	Yard crafts
Beadwork	Nautical crafts
Decoupage	Model making
Plastics and acrylics	Glassblowing

Quick Quiz for the Home-Based Artisan

Before getting down to business, as it were, let's see if you've got the stuff to manage your own craft business. Answer yes or no to the following questions.

	Yes	No
1. Are you a self-starter?	___	___
2. Are you willing to work harder and longer than you ever imagined?	___	___
3. Do you work well without supervision?	___	___
4. Do you work well under pressure?	___	___
5. Are you able to organize details?	___	___
6. Can you take charge of projects and see them through to completion?	___	___
7. Do you have an independent nature?	___	___
8. Do you consider yourself well disciplined?	___	___
9. Are you willing to make sacrifices to succeed?	___	___
10. Do you consider honesty important in business?	___	___
11. Do you assume all your business dealings will be with honest people?	___	___
12. Do you mind seeing to menial chores?	___	___
13. Do you work best as a team member?	___	___
14. Are you a procrastinator?	___	___
15. Do you think work has to be fun?	___	___
16. Are you a creative person?	___	___
17. Can you be stern with people who owe you money?	___	___
18. Do you consider it necessary to meet or beat all deadlines?	___	___
19. Do you have a firm grasp of the basics of your chosen craft(s)?	___	___
20. Do you own sufficient and adequate craft-making equipment?	___	___

	Yes	No
21. Do you own as much craft-making equipment as you'll ever need?	____	____
22. Do you know as much about crafts as you'll ever need to know?	____	____
23. Is the camaraderie of coworkers necessary?	____	____
24. Do you feel that strict follow-up procedures are a waste of time?	____	____
25. Are peer recognition and praise essential to your success and happiness?	____	____

If you answered *yes* to questions 1 through 10, *no* to 11 through 15, *yes* to 16 through 20, and *no* to 21 through 25, why aren't you already running your own home-based craft business?

Don't fret if you have some *yes* answers where *no* answers belong, or vice versa. This test was designed to provide a quick self-evaluation and to call to your attention some of the realities of being a self-employed artisan and manager. You may have discovered one weakness or several areas you need to work on, or attitudes that need adjusting.

02

Working Out of Your Home

During much of the twentieth century, the trend for most Americans was to live in one place and work in another. In recent years, however, increasing numbers of people have moved back to their homes to do business. Studies by the U.S. Small Business Administration (SBA) have indicated that more than 627,000 home-based businesses were launched in 2008. About 126,000 are craft businesses.

Several technological advancements have combined to allow people the increased freedom of working at home. Certainly, the development of the personal computer must head the list. Reinforcing the advent of the home computer is the establishment of modern communications including the Internet, e-mail, websites, blogs, fax machines, etc. The information super-highway has revolutionized the way global cartels, major corporations, small businesses, and individual entrepreneurs communicate, interact, and conduct their business.

Augmenting all these technological advances was the establishment of nationwide networks of rapid delivery and courier services. The U.S. Postal Service offers Express Mail overnight delivery to most destinations within the United States. United Parcel Service guarantees next-day delivery with its "Red Label" service, second-day delivery of the cheaper "Blue Label" parcels, and three-day delivery that's cheaper yet. Similar services are available at competitive prices from other companies, such as FedEx. It's now possible to send a letter, proposal, price sheet, report, manuscript, or stack of documents coast to coast faster than it took to get a document across town thirty years ago.

The attraction of working at home has enticed many of us to go into business for ourselves. Working where we live allows us to avoid long, time-wasting commutes and reduces wear and tear on our vehicles. We're able to escape the hassles of office politics and personality conflicts with bosses and peers. We can dodge all the nonproductive meetings and work at our own improved pace. We can also arrange flexible schedules to accommodate a variety of needs.

The Pros and Cons of Self-Employment

For most of us who have been in business a while, the advantages of home-based self-employment far outweigh the disadvantages. You ought to know at the outset, though, that some people just don't take to this kind of life. So approach your business cautiously and weigh the options carefully.

I get the impression from people I talk to that the two qualities most people either think or fear they lack are self-motivation and self-discipline. These two attributes work hand in hand and are essential to the success of any home-based business, but they are realities you simply must face, not fears that should put you off unnecessarily. Of course, you must be motivated. Of course, you must be disciplined. But so must you be to hold a job, to get to work on time, to show up for appointments, to take responsibility for projects, to see to family business, to be a dependable person, to be a good friend.

The move from passenger to pilot can seem a quantum leap, but it needn't be frightening. You'll have to reach inside yourself to find the required character traits, but outside influences may be even greater motivators. When people ask me how I can get up every morning and go to work without giving in to the temptation to sleep in or take the day off and go fishing, I tell them it's easy: I have a natural aversion to poverty, hunger, and failure.

All of us are tempted from time to time, and on rare occasions we even give in. It's human nature, and there's nothing wrong with that. What you can't afford to do, however, is to make a habit of succumbing to all the diversions and thereby jeopardize deadlines and other commitments. To do so is to risk your reputation—indeed, your business.

If sleeping in or taking a day or afternoon off might cause you to miss a deadline, then don't do it. If, on the other hand, you've been working hard and a little time off will do no harm, then the decision is up to you. Keep in mind, though, that when you miss a morning, an afternoon, or an entire day, all your business activities screech to a halt; the work won't get done in your absence. You might have to put in some evenings or weekend time to catch up. So every time you're tempted, ask yourself if it's worth it.

On the other hand, when you finish a full day's work by noon, you can keep working to get ahead of schedule, or take the afternoon off with no pangs of guilt. Likewise, when you occasionally wrap up a week's work on Thursday instead of Friday, you should have no compunction about rewarding yourself with a three-day weekend.

The All-Collar Worker

At a conference I attended several years ago, an economist talked about blue-collar and white-collar workers, then told the audience about no-collar workers. "I'm talking about people who wear T-shirts or sweatshirts, Levi's, and running shoes," he said. "They work at home, and they represent the fastest-growing segment of the workforce." He was referring to the millions of Americans who work full-time from their homes. Some are home-based employees of corporations, while the rest are in business for themselves.

Although his facts and figures were interesting, his labeling was all wrong. In our home-based businesses, each of us runs the gamut from chief executive to laborer. I make all the important administrative and creative decisions in my business, but I also order the office supplies, make the coffee, vacuum the carpet, sweep up the shop, dust the filing cabinets and bookshelves, put off the filing, and wish someone would wash the windows. If anything, I'm an all-collar worker.

No More Nine-to-Five Grind

Many persons who aspire to the independence of running a home-based business dream of the day when they can chuck the daily routine: no more Monday-through-Friday, nine-to-five grind. That's true. Your home-based craft business will probably require a Monday-through-Saturday schedule, with plenty of Sundays thrown in. Instead of slugging away from nine to five, you'll probably be hard at it from six to six and might have to work some evenings to keep up.

No More Bosses

Similarly, those who think being their own boss is the greatest benefit of being self-employed are in for some surprises. The idea of any craft business is to have customers, and plenty of them. Your job is to please your customers. In a sense, then, every customer is your boss. Depending on the nature of your business, you might have orders to fill, commissions to complete, fairs and exhibits to attend—in other words, a life as full of deadlines as any job you may have had before starting your own business.

So if you are thinking of going into business because you don't like following your boss's orders or you hate the pressure of incessant deadlines, you're doing it for the wrong reasons. As a self-employed artisan, you must honor your commitments to countless people, and you must meet their deadlines. To do otherwise is to court peril.

Isolation—Curse or Blessing?

Isolation is also something every home-based artisan must deal with. Oddly, the reality of it comes as a surprise to many people who decide to run businesses from their homes. Some are truly distraught by being cut off from the daily interaction with others, particularly those who leave busy jobs where isolation is rare or nonexistent. The rest of us revel in the solitude and the high level of productivity it fosters.

If most of your business is local, you will come in contact with more people than if the bulk of your work is for distant clients. Even in the latter case, you'll need to stay in touch with people by phone, mail, e-mail, and through the occasional business trip, trade show, association meeting, or craft fair.

If your craft business is one that requires meetings with clients, you might consider luncheon meetings as a way of getting away from home for an hour or so. This can be a refreshing diversion if you don't mind dividing your workday to allow it. Breakfast meetings can be a good alternative for people who don't like to break up their workdays.

Artisans who sell their products mainly at craft fairs and arts-and-crafts exhibits rarely get to know their customers. Even if you sell regularly to local or regional galleries and gift shops, most of your clients will probably remain casual acquaintances with whom you're not inclined to lunch. So if you feel the need to get away from your home or to engage in conversation, take a lunch break with a friend or spouse. You might even plan these luncheons to be regular, if not frequent, diversions.

Two self-employed friends of mine make it a point to have lunch together once or twice a month as a way of getting out of the house and having a conversation with someone who's not a customer or family member. They've gone so far as to set up a lunch fund to which each contributes. That way, no one's responsible for the tab or tip, and they feel as if neither has to pay for lunch. Little games like this tend to open pressure valves and help make running a business more enjoyable.

Setting Up Your Business Space

One of the first orders of business is to plan, design, and set up your work space. This is a matter of both logistics and legalities. Your business will require a certain amount of space. Your home may or may not impose space restrictions on your business. In order to qualify as a legitimate business for tax purposes, the space you set aside will have to meet certain criteria. (See chapter 8 under "Using Your Home as a Business.")

The advantages of converting part of your home to a work space far outweigh the alternative, which is to rent or lease business space. Commercial spaces rent for as little as $10 a square foot per month in smaller towns, to as high as $32 a square foot, especially in large cities. You won't burn out any brain cells calculating the minimum of $1,500 a month you'll save by converting a 10-by-15-foot spare room into a home office instead of renting one downtown.

Just to rent the commercial equivalent of my office, studio, darkroom, and workshop would cost me more than $2,300 a month, or nearly four times my monthly mortgage payment. What's more, I get an annual tax deduction for that part of my home devoted entirely to the operation of my business.

How and where you go about setting up your work space is entirely up to you and depends largely on the space available and how you intend to operate. Obviously, if your business is solely devoted to needlecraft, you won't need a big workshop full of expensive woodworking tools. If you're both an artist and an artisan, perhaps one room will serve as both studio and workshop. If your office is big enough, it might also double as a studio or workroom. A large closet can become a storeroom. You can convert a garage or outbuilding into a warehouse.

Every home-based entrepreneur, however, needs a place to conduct business: to see to correspondence, accounts payable, accounts receivable, the endless flow of paperwork, and all the other business chores. Whether this turns out to be one end of the dining-room table, a desk in a corner of a bedroom, or a full-fledged home office depends on what you need and what's available.

One of the beauties of the home-based craft business is that you can start small. Even if your chosen craft is relatively expensive, you probably won't need as much equipment and materials as you would in another kind of business. Consequently, your start-up costs can be comparatively low. Depending on what you already own and how good you are at scrounging and improvising, you should be able to break into the business for somewhere between a few hundred and a few thousand dollars—certainly less than five thousand.

As mentioned previously, you need to set up some sort of office space, and while there's nothing wrong with using part of another room in your home, you may not claim that space as a home office when you file your tax return. Any space you set up in your home for the purpose of running a business must be used *regularly* and *exclusively* for that business if you are going to claim a deduction for it. That means it must be a separate room or rooms. If you don't have separate facilities available, so be it.

If you can, though, try to convert any available rooms, add on, or plan for the additional space the next time you move or build. It's better not only for tax purposes, but also for doing business and keeping your business and personal life separate. You will have a discrete, clearly defined place to go to work, to conduct business, and, above all, to leave at the end of the workday.

As in any other planning operation, you need to put this information on paper. You should write out your wants and needs and sketch out floor plans that will accommodate your physical requirements.

You can operate a craft business from any kind of dwelling. Since my part-time beginnings, I have run my business from an apartment, two log cabins, a town house, a rental house, and finally from the house I live in now, which was designed to include comfortable living quarters on one level and my business complex on the other level.

When I started my business, my wife and I lived in a two-bedroom apartment. I was able to set up one bedroom as my office and makeshift studio. Although I was able to design woodworking projects in the comfort of my office/studio, I had to see to the labor outdoors, where I set up a temporary workbench with a slab of plywood on two sawhorses.

We had a similar situation at the town house we rented when we moved to the Oregon coast. There, though, a private patio served as my outdoor workshop. When it rained, I moved my work to the kitchen. Adjacent to the kitchen and next to the sliding door to the patio was a large closet with bifold doors, which I converted into a compact workshop and storage area.

One of the two bedrooms on the second floor of the town house served as my office and studio. It was a separate room that I used exclusively and regularly for business purposes and was therefore deductible as a home office. The patio and kitchen, however, were temporary work spaces, not used exclusively for business purposes, so they did not qualify for any kind of deduction.

I did not take a deduction for the large closet I had converted, for which I can only plead stupidity. For some reason, it never occurred to me that I could—after all, it was just a closet. It was not functioning as a closet, however. It was a separate room, with doors closing it off from other rooms. I used it exclusively and regularly for business purposes. So it qualified for a legitimate deduction I failed to take. Don't make the same kind of mistake.

There never seems to be enough storage room, so plan accordingly. When we moved into the town house, I got along fine for about a year, but then I had to rent additional storage space. When we built the house we now occupy, we planned carefully and thought we'd never run out of space. We have used up all that space, however, and have once again had to rent a storage unit to house the overflow.

In planning the physical structure of your business, pay close attention to your equipment requirements. List your immediate needs for each aspect of your business and note how you intend to fill them. You might also list your mid-range and long-term needs. If you answered the series of ten questions near the beginning of chapter 1, you have already made such a list in response to question 5. Following are some hints that may help you in this process.

The Home Office

If your home business is a craft business, you may forget that a home office will be an essential part of conducting an efficient and professional enterprise.

With that in mind, take the time to consider this aspect of your home-based business and setting up your home office with the necessary accoutrements, including a desk, chair, filing cabinet, wastebasket, telephone, and computer with Internet service.

You will probably want a bookcase or bookshelves, and perhaps a storage cabinet of some sort. Select the office supplies you find useful. As you become more experienced with running the office side of your business, you will be able to determine what else is necessary and what is not.

Just as you should plan for more storage space than you think you'll need, try to design as much horizontal working surface as possible into your home office. Desktops are never large enough, and they act like magnets for clutter. So plan for more surface space than a single desk offers, perhaps with the addition of a worktable, a credenza, or even a second desk.

I have two desks in my office. A conventional desk stands in the middle of the room, and another behind it functions as a computer station. Other furniture and fixtures in my office include two-drawer and four-drawer filing cabinets, a wall of bookshelves, an AM-FM stereo, and a cuckoo clock for company—birds of a feather, I guess.

The Home Studio

A studio is many things to many people and can be anything you want to make it. It's probably the most variable room of all among home-based artists and artisans. You may not need one at all, but if you do, you must determine how you will use it in order to know how much space you need and how you will furnish it. My studio would be more than some people might need but woefully inadequate for others.

I knew when I designed my work complex that I needed a fair-sized multipurpose room, which, for lack of a better name, I called my studio. It's a rectangular room, 13 by 18 feet. One end of it functions as a photography studio, but the room does much more than that. Four-drawer filing cabinets line one wall, and floor-to-ceiling bookshelves run the length of two others. So this is also my research and reference library.

Permanent furniture includes a desk, a chair, and a large worktable. Atop the desk are dozens of labeled file trays that initially sort the mountain of paperwork associated with running my home-based business. So the studio is also where I do most of my filing.

Woodworking is a major part of my business, but I also do a good bit of picture framing. Although I build and finish frames in my workshop, I see to the rest of the framing process in my studio, simply because framing requires a relatively dust-free environment, which no woodworking shop provides.

Before we built the house we currently occupy, my studio and office were in the same room, and I got along adequately with that arrangement. As my business grew, I soon realized that I would need much more space than any single room might provide, and that was my motivation for having separate office and studio/library facilities.

The Home Workshop

A workshop is another room you may or may not need, depending on the kind of craft you create. This is a province for the messy crafts, and you might call this work space a workshop, workroom, or studio. In my case, it's clearly a workshop, full of hand tools, portable and stationary power tools, and woodworking materials.

My next-door neighbor is a woodcarver who works in his garage, which is also full of hand tools, portable and stationary power tools, and woodworking materials. He calls his work space a studio, and I wouldn't quibble with that nomenclature. He's more artist than artisan, and I'm the opposite. My shop and his studio are similar because of the medium we work in and the fact that each of us regularly dabbles in the other's realm.

My shop is 24 by 24 feet and is comfortable and adequate for creating a great variety of woodcraft projects. Storage has become a problem in recent years. Consequently, in addition to renting storage space, I'm continually reorganizing my work complex to relieve the burden that has befallen both my shop and studio.

Keep this in mind as you design your own work space. Try to allow for more room than you think you'll need. As your business prospers and grows, however, your work space will begin bulging at the seams. That may be a good time to reassess your needs and possibly redesign and expand your business space.

The Home Warehouse

As I mentioned earlier, you're going to need plenty of storage space—probably more than you think—and at times you may need more than usual. Building inventory to prepare for the upcoming tourist season or Christmas-shopping season can put a strain on your storage facilities, as can stockpiling for an arts-and-crafts fair.

Part of your workshop or studio may suffice. You might temporarily have to use an attic or another room in your house, but remember, if you don't use that room regularly and exclusively for business purposes, it is not eligible for a tax deduction.

Another option is to rent or lease storage space temporarily at one of the mini–storage facilities available in most communities. If you use this space exclusively for storing your products and other business-related items, you can deduct the rent as a business expense.

If you regularly travel the craft-fair and trade-show circuits and find you have a relatively permanent problem with storing inventory, you should consider converting another room, adding on, or putting up a separate facility to function as a permanent home-business warehouse.

Extra Hands

When considering your work space, keep in mind that as your business expands you may need additional labor. How will you accommodate this? One option is to bring in full-time, part-time, or temporary help. But you don't necessarily need to make space for people to work with you at your home. See "Handling Growth" in chapter 10 for a discussion of the various options.

Separating Business Life from Personal Life

I have read that it's impossible for the home-based entrepreneur to keep business life and personal life separate. To the extent that no business or job can be kept entirely isolated from personal and family affairs, I would agree. But it's essential for the success of your business and your overall well-being that you make every effort to keep the two distinct and apart.

If you have a family, your home-based business is going to affect it in some way, and vice versa. If your business is only in the preliminary planning stages, waste no time in bringing certain family members on board and making clear to them what your plans are and how they might affect family life. A spouse should be part of your planning from the start. You may want to postpone discussing the venture with young children until you're ready to launch the business, but you should talk with older children early on.

Moreover, you must make it clear to your family, friends, and neighbors that although you will be working at home in your new business, you are indeed working, and during work hours you are not available for chores, babysitting, ball playing, shopping, shuttle service, or anything else not related to your craft business.

For some baffling reason, people tend to think that a person who works at home isn't really working. Consequently, you can count on them to try to impose on you in every imaginable way. Friends, neighbors, and even family members will think nothing of phoning or dropping in during business hours just to chat, when they would never dream of doing such a thing to a chef, a physician, a teacher, or an auto mechanic who works away from home.

Sometimes home-based entrepreneurs get what they ask for—no respect. I've heard of some who delight in the fact that they're able to work at home all day in robe and slippers. I can't imagine taking my business seriously, or expecting others to, while lounging around all day in bed clothing. I certainly can't entertain or meet with clients so attired. And what are drop-ins and coffee klatchers to think if I greet them at the door in pajamas and try to convince them I'm busy?

Of course, I might catch up on paperwork late at night in the bedroom. I often see to early-morning phone calls during my first cup of coffee, before I've showered and donned my work duds. When it's time for business, however, I'm dressed for it.

It's also important for your business image and peace of mind that you establish a business routine. You must have operating days and hours, and you must make these known to family, friends, and neighbors. Otherwise, they'll be all too quick to assume you're not really working.

Marketing Your Craft Business

The thorniest dilemma any crafter faces is getting the word out that your product is for sale. So let's take a moment to look at your options before getting into the nuts and bolts of setting up your business. After all, knowing how to close a sale won't do you any good unless you can initiate that sale to begin with—and you can't do that without marketing.

Marketing is what you do to create interest in your product and place it in the hands of potential customers. It can include sales, public relations, packaging, and pricing.

Although marketing and selling are inextricably interrelated, selling is but one part of the marketing process. Selling is the exchange of merchandise for cash; marketing encompasses all aspects of the transfer of goods from manufacturer to consumer. A sound marketing program includes promotion, public relations, and customer service, as well as the storage, sales, and shipment of products.

Marketing is your ultimate purpose and should be part of every phase of your business. It precedes the manufacture and transcends the sale of merchandise. First, last, and always, your business is marketing.

Creating a Marketable Reputation

The magnitude of the marketing effort surprises many fledgling entrepreneurs. It's a big and important job that takes a lot of time and effort, especially in the beginning. Much of it amounts to researching and finding potential customers, then building a sound and salable reputation. During the early stages of your business, all this might consume more than half your time.

When I started my business as a part-timer, I wasn't wholly prepared for the task and for how my time would be divided. I was naive enough to think I could spend countless hours creating masterpieces, then devote any time left to the more mundane matters of managing a business and marketing my work. In short, I saw these chores as spare-time tasks.

After a severe attack of reality, I realized I was spending about 80 percent of my time managing and marketing my business and 20 percent in creative pursuits. Meanwhile, though, I was also establishing a marketable reputation that would eventually enable me to improve that ratio.

No matter what sort of craft(s) you're engaged in, your most important product is professionalism. You must establish a reputation for reliability, competence, punctuality, courtesy, superior services, sacred deadlines, and guaranteed satisfaction.

Market Analysis

As a home-based entrepreneur, you can't afford to conduct surveys and market analysis the way major corporations do, but you should develop a solid notion of who and where your customers are and what they're looking for.

The problem is, too many artisans get it backward. They manufacture products first, then try to find buyers for them. It must be the other way around: Research the marketplace; then develop products that will sell there.

In the home-based craft business, the key to successful market analysis is observation. You must pay close attention to how and where craft products are sold, what prices other artisans charge for their products, and who buys them.

Product Salability

If there's one common blind spot crafters possess, it's the inability to admit that others may not like your craft.

This is not as uncommon as you may think. In our enthusiasm for a particular craft, we may attempt to project our fervor onto buyers and then feel frustrated when customers are not as keen to part with their cash as we feel they should be. Nonetheless we keep trying to beat a dead horse and make it run. We continue attending craft fairs and other selling venues, attempting to force customers to recognize the merit of our product.

If this sounds familiar, it's time to stop and take a deep breath. After endless failed attempts to garner customer interest in a craft, you'll be forced to reach one of three possible conclusions: (1) you're marketing your craft to the wrong audience; (2) there's something wrong with your craft (workmanship, color, price, etc.); or (3) your craft just isn't salable.

If the issue is salability, don't give up hope. In a best-case scenario, it may just take a few tweaks to increase consumer interest. In the worst case, you'll have to take the skills and tools you already have and apply your talents to a different product line. With time, this ability to roll with the punches often translates into outstanding success as a crafter because you're giving the customer what *he* wants, not what *you* want him to have.

Find the Right Outlets

In order to determine who will buy your products, you must first decide where your best sales outlets are. Here are some possibilities:

- Gift and souvenir shops
- Arts-and-crafts galleries
- Specialty shops
- Chain stores
- Craft malls
- Mail-order outlets
- Arts-and-crafts co-ops
- Aquarium and museum gift shops
- Craft fairs
- Wholesale trade shows
- Retail trade shows
- Festivals and bazaars
- Sidewalk arts-and-crafts exhibits
- Farmers' markets
- Flea markets and swap meets
- Powwows and potlatches
- Vendor carts and booths
- Food and beverage festivals
- Open houses and craft parties
- The World Wide Web

Start Small and Market Locally

Learn about every possible nearby outlet. Determine what's available in your town, in your county, and within easy driving distance of your home. Find out where and when all the craft fairs and related exhibits are in your community and in nearby towns. Similarly, identify and locate all the shops and galleries that might handle your products. These should be your primary marketing targets.

Gradually extend your research to include potential sales outlets throughout your state and region. Take some scouting trips and check out all the shops and galleries.

In every town you visit, your first stop should be the local chamber of commerce or visitor center. Collect general descriptive literature about the community and find out about all the local events that offer opportunities for craft sales. Most chambers and visitor centers have brochures and other publications that provide all the details you need. Be sure to get literature about shopping, restaurants, and lodging, and ask for a complimentary copy of the local phone directory. Back home, file this material for later reference and trip planning.

Tell the person at the visitor center what you're up to and ask for recommendations. Sometimes potential outlets exist in the least likely places.

On Oregon's north coast, for example, is the small town of Tillamook in a sparsely populated county of the same name. Since shortly after pioneer settlement, this has been dairy country. In fact, the county is home to about 25,000 people and 50,000 cows. At the north end of town, on the main highway, is a large industrial-looking building and a sign over it that reads TILLAMOOK CREAMERY ASSOCIATION. It's known locally as "the cheese factory" and would seem a more likely place to find Kraft products than craft products.

Nevertheless, about half the complex is devoted to tourist facilities, including a restaurant, deli, soda fountain, and wine shop. Nearly a million tourists stop here each year and take the popular tour of the cheese factory. They emerge from the industrial end of the complex into a large sales area, where they can buy all kinds of cheese products as well as books, gifts, and craft items. It's the second-largest man-made tourist attraction on the Oregon coast and a tremendous sales outlet for artisans with the right products.

During your scouting trips you'll learn about many other places you might not normally consider to be possible sales outlets. In my travels, I've found gift shops and galleries at hotels, motels, and lodges. I've been surprised to find artworks and craft items on sale at a good many restaurants, marinas, and even campgrounds and RV parks.

Make the most of your trips. Ask the locals lots of questions. Take copious notes. And observe, observe, observe.

Selling to Shops and Galleries

When I started in business as a part-time entrepreneur, I sold my work through a gallery in Fairbanks called The Alaska House. In those days the standard shop or gallery markup was 50 percent of wholesale or 33.3 percent of retail, meaning that two-thirds of the retail price was my share and one-third went to the shop or gallery. So if I sold a product for $10 or $100, it got marked up to $15 or $150 (or usually $14.95 or $149.50).

Now the markup is 100 percent of wholesale, or at least it is where I live. That means shop and gallery owners simply double the wholesale price and keep half for themselves. Some markups are even higher, particularly if the artisan has underpriced the products.

A couple of years ago, my next-door neighbor began making resin castings of his wood carvings to sell through gift shops. He figured $19.95 would be a good retail price for his cast whales, so he wholesaled them at $10 each. I tried to tell him he was underpricing his work, but he was reluctant to charge more, until I returned from one of my trips to report that I'd found his resin whales on sale for $39.95—a 300 percent markup.

The time to approach shop and gallery owners is not when customers are standing in line to pay for their purchases. Plan your scouting trips for the off-season, if possible, so that you can talk to proprietors at their leisure. Ask them about the possibility of selling your work through them and find out when they normally do their buying.

Keep in mind that in most places of business (gift shops, galleries, etc.), sales clerks are *not* store buyers. They have no say in whether or not the establishment will carry a product, beyond mentioning your craft to management. If you're pushy or persistent, they're less likely to be cooperative. Cornering hapless clerks is counterproductive because (a) they *don't* make the buying decisions, and (b) *no one* likes to be pushed. Your best bet might be to make an appointment with the manager or store buyer, rather than trying to convince the sales clerk that the store should carry your craft.

If you're not familiar with local customs and don't know when the buying and selling seasons are, ask other local artists and artisans. Where I live, summer is a big selling season. Store buyers generally order stock from late winter to late spring, but some shop and gallery owners set aside only a few weeks to buy for the coming season. The owners of one of my favorite galleries do all their budgeting in January and buy all their stock in February. The artist or artisan who shows up in March hoping to sell to these folks is out of luck.

September and October are usually busy buying times for shop and gallery buyers stocking for the coming holiday season. After Christmas things are pretty slow where I live. Elsewhere—in the Southwest or deep South, for example—tourism is at its peak at that time. So you'll have to find out on your own what the seasons are in your part of the country. If you plan to travel and sell outside your region, take the climatic differences into account.

Craft Fairs and Trade Shows

Craft fairs are often held at shopping malls, armories, high school gymnasiums, community centers, and other facilities that provide adequate display space and parking. Some are juried and require potential exhibitors to submit samples of their work to a committee that determines whether the products are of sufficient quality. Others let space to anyone who can come up with the fees.

Local craft fairs are great places for artisans new to the business to get involved with a minimal investment. Some fairs, especially those in the larger metropolitan areas, are excellent sales outlets for neophytes and veterans alike.

Fees for the smaller local weekend fairs usually range from $25 to $125. Promoters of the big shows on the national circuit can demand $200 to $500 or more and have no problem filling spaces.

Retail trade shows are usually held in coliseums, stadiums, convention centers, fairgrounds, and other places that have the capacity to hold large crowds. They're open to the public and are thematic in nature. Craft professionals interested in exhibiting at these big shows need to match their products with the show themes and should expect to pay from $300 to as much as $1,500 in exhibit fees.

Wholesale trade shows are closed to the public. This is where manufacturers' reps, business owners, professional buyers, industry media, and others gather for big-time marketing. These shows can be huge, such as the one I attended several summers ago at Chicago's McCormick Place, where there were nearly sixty acres of exhibits displaying the products of 3,000 companies. Of all the shows, these are the least likely to be of value to home-based craft professionals.

Susan Ratliff has written a dandy little book for persons interested in knowing more about craft fairs and trade shows. It's called *How to Be a Weekend Entrepreneur: Making Money at Craft Fairs and Trade Shows*. I happily recommend it.

Dress for Success

Keep in mind that you're selling yourself as well as your products. Whether you're calling on a shop owner or staffing a booth at a craft fair, dress for success. That doesn't necessarily mean you must look like a Fortune 500 CEO, but you ought to present the appearance of a successful professional. Demonstrate that you have good taste and judgment by dressing well for the occasion in clothes of good quality.

Appearance isn't everything, but it can make a big difference to some of the people to whom you hope to sell your products. Scruffy attire can imply sloppy craftsmanship and careless business practices. A good appearance, on the other hand, has never cost anyone a sale.

Hiring a Rep

Some craft professionals don't need or want the services of sales representatives; others swear they can't get by without them. You'll have to decide for yourself. If you detest dealing directly with shop and gallery owners, or if you would rather spend most of your time on the creative aspects of your business and leave the sales to someone else, you're a good candidate for a rep.

Sales reps can be indispensable for artisans who want to place their work nationally. Reps who attend the big shows can write a lot of orders, so if you're aspiring toward a high level of production, consider representation.

Reps function as independent contractors and are paid a percentage of the sales they make for you—usually 10 to 15 percent. Some also charge for show expenses.

You'll be expected to sign an agency agreement or contract, which you may want your attorney to review. Remember that contracts should be mutually beneficial to both parties and that much of what appears in any such agreement ought to be negotiable.

Ask local craft professionals whether they're represented, and if so, what they think of their reps. That's one way to find a rep to handle your work. Another way is to ask proprietors of gift shops and art galleries for recommendations.

Consignment

"Consignment" means you give your crafts products to a store, which holds them until a sale is made. It's the business's job to keep your products safe from breakage, theft, or ruin, as well as put them on display and attract buyers. They then take a portion of the sale price for the effort it took to store, promote, and sell your products.

In theory, consignment stores only make money when they make a sale, and therein lies their motivation.

There are a number of issues in consignment sales that need to be crystal clear before you hand over your products. How long does the store anticipate it will take to sell your items? What is the split between you and the store? How will the merchandise be safeguarded, displayed, and advertised? Who is responsible if any of your products are damaged or stolen? How long will it take you to get paid for an item?

The trouble with a consignment situation is you lose control of your sales as well as your products. All the control is in the hands of the seller. Be sure to read *all* the fine print in the consignment contract.

There is a natural conflict of interest that occurs in a consignment situation as opposed to a regular retail relationship. Crafters want a higher percentage of profits and a decent selling price. Store owners want the crafter to accept a lower percentage of profits, and they want to price the items lower in order to move them faster. There's a different motivation if a store purchases your craft items outright through a wholesale purchase. They have already laid out the money, and therefore they must recoup their expenses as rapidly as possibly. That is an excellent incentive to sell. But if they haven't laid out any money for their inventory, their motivation is less urgent—to the crafter's detriment.

Remember, patience is a highly underappreciated aspect of consignment sales. If you are not in any hurry to receive money for your craft, then working in a few consignment situations to round out your sales can be beneficial. If you have stock sitting on a shelf and nowhere to market it, you might as well do *something* with it. However, if you think you'll get rich doing consignments, think again.

Publicity and Promotion

Publicity is the kind of advertising money can't buy. Advertising, which we'll discuss at greater length in the coming pages, is a concentrated and focused effort that you pay for and exercise some control over. Although you can and should guide publicity and control it as best you can, you might not have the final word here; someone else probably will.

Publicity has the same goal as advertising—to get your business known and recognized by potential clients or customers—but is accomplished in different ways. Good publicity is far more valuable than advertising for the very reason that it *isn't* paid for. Consequently, it seems more like an unsolicited endorsement, which it often is.

It's important to get your name before the public at every opportunity. As with advertising, the greatest effects of publicity are cumulative, so it's equally important to keep your name and business image prominent and visible to potential customers.

Organizations

A number of organizations can assist you in a variety of ways. National professional and business associations can offer helpful hints and provide a useful exchange of ideas. Association with your peers across the nation can lead to important business contacts.

Local business, fraternal, and other organizations can also do much to publicize and promote your business and put you in touch with people you need to know: likely customers or business associates. I met and got to know both my attorney and my insurance agent when the three of us worked as committee members for a local chapter of a national conservation organization. I also made other significant contacts through the same association. Donating my time and work to the organization got my business a good bit of publicity as well.

Some associations worth investigating are your local chamber of commerce, Jaycees, Junior League, Lion's Club, Rotary, and Kiwanis. And don't overlook the special interest clubs and associations, some of which are listed in the "Source Directory" at the back of this book.

Media Publicity

A little media publicity can go a long way toward getting your name and business reputation known in your community. What's more, capturing local media attention might be a lot easier than you think.

Newspapers of all sizes run business profiles and features on local entrepreneurs. Small-town and suburban weeklies are the surest bets, but dailies also use such stories.

Visit the newspaper offices in your area, and talk to the appropriate business editor, features editor, managing editor, or whoever assigns such stories. Keep in mind that it's best to have an angle or "peg" for the story.

Perhaps you have an interest or specialty that will add appeal to a story about your business. Do you use any unusual techniques, materials, or equipment in your craft business? If you use any locally manufactured or regionally indigenous natural materials, that can be of particular interest. Do you work with traditional materials and ancient processes? Is there a local historical peg to your business and its story? At the other end of the spectrum, perhaps you work with the latest high-tech equipment to create products for the twenty-first century.

Local radio and television stations often air interview and talk shows that can prove good sources of publicity. TV stations might even want to film your products, or perhaps show you at work creating your crafts. Don't miss an opportunity like this one.

Public Relations

Another way to exploit print and electronic media is with public relations (PR) techniques. For instance, you can use news releases to get the word out about you and your business, but you should have a good news peg to make your release irresistible.

News releases differ from the kind of publicity discussed earlier in that you furnish the copy to the media. You generate the story, either by writing it yourself or hiring someone to write it.

There's nothing wrong with writing your own news releases, providing you possess the necessary skills. If you can't tell a semicolon from a semiconductor, however, get help.

Some editors will use your releases with little or no modification. Others might follow up with phone calls to augment the material you furnish. Still others might assign a reporter and photographer to do a feature or photo spread.

Even if there's nothing particularly unusual or exciting about your business, you can still use public relations to your advantage. Special events, awards, and honors are always good news pegs. So when you win "best of show" at a juried exhibition or take three blue ribbons at the county fair, make sure your local print and electronic media people know about it. When a professional association elects you to high office or presents you with an award, get out a news release.

It is helpful to utilize modern media opportunities (such as blogs, Facebook, and Twitter) in your public relations efforts. Facebook allows you to keep interested followers abreast of all your news—where you'll be making appearances, what gallery just agreed to carry your pieces, etc. It is simply another networking tool that can spread the word that your products are available. It goes without saying that your Facebook page should remain *strictly* professional—no risqué photos or juicy tidbits of information should ever be posted!

Twitter is an abbreviated-format communications device that allows you to "tweet" information of up to 140 characters to customers, friends, or colleagues. It is a more immediate way to stay connected with potential clients since the message must be short, sweet, and to the point—and are frequently received on the ubiquitous cell phone.

News Release Format

News releases should follow a standard format that includes all pertinent information. You can use plain white paper or your letterhead. You might want to design a news release form that incorporates your logo.

Make sure your business name, address, phone number, website, and e-mail address appear prominently at the top of the page. The words *News Release* should also appear in large boldface type near the top of the page. Also include the current date, release date, length, and the name and contact info of the person to go to for further information.

For releases going to print media, provide the length, expressed as an approximate number of words. It's best to keep releases brief—usually no more than 200 to 300 words, never more than 500.

Releases for the electronic media should be shorter yet, with length expressed in seconds. You'll have to read them aloud at a normal broadcast pace and time them. Try to confine them to thirty seconds. You can also provide several versions of the same release running different lengths—say, twenty, thirty, and forty seconds. The recipient can then pick whichever one fits an available time slot.

The release date can be the same as the date you prepared and mailed the release, or some later date tied to an event. Your release might have a limited life or time span, which you should indicate on the release date line. For example, if the release should run only during the month of July, the release date should be July 1 through July 31.

Below the information lines, immediately preceding the text of the release, center a title, headline, or description of contents.

If a release requires more than one page, all pages except the first should be numbered sequentially and should carry an abbreviated title at the top. At the

News Release

Crafts Unlimited
1492 Columbus Drive
Moon Valley, IN 54321
(123) 555-4545
www.craftsunlimitedmoonvalley.com
terry@craftsunlimitedmoonvalley.com

To: _____   Date: _____

_____   Length: _____

Release Date :_____   Contact: Terry Johnson,
Owner/Manager

Title, Headline, or Topic

(more)

bottom of every page except the last, enclose the word *more* inside parentheses. At the end of the text, two spaces beneath the final paragraph, center the words *The End* or the symbols # # #.

Use simple sentences and short paragraphs. Avoid jargon and technical language. Use what's known as the *inverse pyramid style,* in which you attempt to put all the essential information into the first paragraph or two and the least important material toward the end. That way, an editor can trim it from the end to accommodate space limitations.

Remember the five *W*s and the *H*—Who, What, Where, When, Why, and How—and make sure every release answers each of those questions.

Displays and Donations

The more people who see your work, the greater the cumulative effect, and the better the likelihood that potential customers will think of you when special needs arise. You must take advantage of every opportunity to publicize your craft and business.

Showing Your Work

The obvious places to show craftwork are galleries and museums, but there are other places you shouldn't overlook. Of course, you should try to sell your work to galleries, and you should enter your handicrafts in exhibit competitions. Talk to gallery owners about handling your work and museum curators about sponsoring one-person shows.

Any business or institution with a lobby, great hall, waiting room, or reception area is a potential client or displayer: banks, clinics, hospitals, dental offices, law offices, executive offices, nursing homes, retirement facilities, senior centers, restaurants, hotels, motels, bed-and-breakfast inns, resorts, ski shops, dive shops, and so on.

You should be able to sell a variety of craftworks to these and other establishments. Those who aren't interested in buying often can be persuaded to display a selection of handicrafts in exchange for their decorative value. Others might agree to display and sell your work on consignment.

In my community, a number of banks display original artwork, photography, and handicrafts as a way of helping artists and artisans get their work before the public. One retirement complex regularly sponsors and publicizes art, craft, and photographic exhibits. Restaurants and resorts up and down the West Coast similarly display the works of local artists, photographers, and artisans.

Donating Your Work

Donating craft items to fund-raisers can also net you some promotional rewards. When a local nonprofit organization sponsors a fund-raising dinner, auction, or sale, the press is sure to cover the event, and you can share the promotional value when you are listed as one of the donors to the cause.

Volunteering Your Time and Skills

Volunteering is another way to reap the rewards of publicity. You can volunteer your time and energies for events sponsored by local nonprofit organizations. The organizations will be grateful for your help, and local media will no doubt help publicize the events, both before and after.

If you can teach what you know about crafts, offer to teach a one-day or weekend craft workshop through a local organization, college, or university. Such a workshop will call for advance publicity in the form of newspaper articles and public service announcements on radio and television.

Advertising Your Business

Whether or not you need to advertise depends largely on the kinds of crafts you're engaged in and the way you normally sell your products. Once you've decided or been advised to advertise, you must determine the best, most cost-effective medium or media.

Should You Hire an Agency?

Advertising is expensive, and advertising agencies are more expensive yet. A good agency can do much for the business ready to use its services but can prove too costly for the new entrepreneur.

A better plan for the start-up home-based craft business is a program that relies primarily on self-promotion, publicity, public relations, and limited advertising. There are media staff people who will work with you on creating ads, and you can do much of the work yourself. First, you must determine what advertising avenues are available in your community or working area, then which will serve you best.

Advertising Media

Advertising takes many shapes and shows up in a variety of places, from the covers of matchbooks to the sides of buses. The media that craft professionals most commonly use include the Yellow Pages, newspapers, magazines, brochures, and specialty advertising. Costs vary widely, as does effectiveness, and each form has its advantages and disadvantages.

■ **Yellow Pages.** This is one of the most basic forms of advertising. It can amount to a simple listing or an elaborate display ad. Staff is available to help you with layout.

Advantages: Directories are widely distributed to everyone who has a phone. People who use the Yellow Pages are in the market for services or products. Directories are kept on hand for a year.
Disadvantages: This is a passive medium, meaning that people can freely choose what ads to read or ignore. Deadline lead times are long. It's seldom a good idea to include price information. The ads are very expensive. And unless you operate a storefront where customers can come see you, a Yellow Page ad may not be worth it.

■ **Newspapers.** The larger the newspaper's circulation, the greater the potential effect of its advertising, but also the higher its advertising rates will be. Nevertheless, newspapers remain among the most used media for localized advertising.

Advantages: Newspapers have a high degree of reader acceptance. Ads are available in a great variety of sizes and can be clipped and saved. They can include as much detail and information as you want or can afford.
Disadvantages: Newspaper ads are relatively expensive. Newspapers are a passive medium and are short-lived (soon discarded). Poor reproduction is a problem at many small newspapers, which will do injustice to any photographs you include with your ads.

■ **Magazines.** Under the right circumstances, magazine advertising can be effective for certain craft businesses. Rates are high, often prohibitive, even in some city and regional magazines.

Advantages: Reproduction is usually superior to that of other print media. Target marketing is most precise. You can include as much detail as you wish, and ads can be clipped and saved.

Disadvantages: Magazines usually have long lead times for deadlines. Like other print media, they are passive and are often so cluttered with ads that readers skip them.

■ **Brochures.** For many crafts, brochures can be an effective form of advertising.

Advantages: Brochures provide the greatest amount of space for detailed information. They offer the opportunity to showcase your creative skills and can function as a portfolio of your work. You can use brochures to reach a targeted direct-mail market. Brochures are fairly easy to create and can be relatively inexpensive to produce.

Disadvantages: Brochures can be time-consuming and expensive to distribute. Those with color photography are expensive to produce.

■ **Specialty Advertising.** This category includes all the promotional paraphernalia such as pens, pencils, letter openers, digital clocks, calendars, buttons, caps, and other products bearing a business logo and advertising message. Most of these gimmicks probably have greater goodwill value than advertising worth.

Advantages: Nobody objects to getting these little freebies. You can target your market, and the advertising value lasts as long as the object.

Disadvantages: Space for advertising is usually very limited. You must buy a large quantity to keep the per-item cost down. Effective distribution can be costly and time-consuming.

Tips on Advertising Effectively

Media staff and your local SBDC can offer helpful hints for getting the most out of your advertising dollar. Meanwhile, here are a few more tips that should help:

■ Make sure all your print ads prominently display your name, address, phone number, e-mail, and website and/or blog URL.

■ Don't make your ads and commercials too busy; keep them concise and uncluttered.

■ Saturday is usually a poor day to advertise in newspapers; Sunday is typically a good day.

- A good way to make newspaper ads last longer is to buy space in a weekend supplement or weekly TV and entertainment guide or section.

The Best Advertising of All

The best advertising is the kind you can't buy. It grows out of your reputation and is spread by people who know your work and freely recommend it. It's often called *word-of-mouth advertising*, a term that leaves the impression that this is a form of exposure that is usually narrow in scope. In practice, however, it's a wonderfully compounding dividend that you collect on the principal of your good reputation.

Internet Marketing

A craft business without a web presence is like a car without gas—it will only go as far as you can physically push it without any of the multiplying benefits from an outside energy source.

A website or blog allows a crafter to reach a much wider audience (including an international one) than the limitations of local or regional craft shows, galleries, or other selling venues. A web presence dissolves borders. It also allows interested buyers to follow your work on a day-to-day basis rather than through a chance once-in-awhile meeting with you, the crafter.

Unlike the wildly complicated methods needed to set up websites or blogs in years past, you can now pull together a handsome, informative site or blog using any number of free online tools and setup options. Typing "free website builders" into a standard search engine will pull up quite a few options. These builders are easy to use (even for the computer illiterate!), and you can personalize your site through the use of premade templates and drag-and-drop building blocks. Some of these free website builders display advertising in the margins (to help subsidize the cost of using their services), while others do not.

Naturally you can also hire a professional webmaster to create a spectacular site with many fancy interactive graphics. However, especially when you're first establishing your craft business, it might be best to keep costs to a minimum, including for your Internet presence. This is where free website builders come in.

You need to recognize what the purpose of your site will be. Is it just informational, allowing prospective buyers to see your wares? If so, using the free options may be your best bet. If you want to take orders through your site, you can connect with PayPal or another online point-of-sale site, as opposed to setting up a specific ISP-provided web sales site. In other words, the massive financial investments and complexities concerning building a retail site may no longer be necessary.

One of the best ways to determine the kind of website or blog you want is to bookmark other sites you admire. What is it about these sites that you find attractive? The layout? The color scheme? The graphics? The ease of use? The overall "look"? Whatever it is, nothing prevents you from duplicating bits and pieces of different websites in order to build your own unique web presence in a way that pleases you and is conducive to attracting customers.

Once you have a site or blog established, it's important to update it regularly. Blogs are especially easy to update, and blog followers come to expect frequent posts to keep abreast of your activities. This is *not* the place to post family chitchat, personal information, or—heaven forbid—risqué photos. It is best to remain utterly professional on the Internet because unprofessional things have a tendency to come back to haunt you.

What about eBay and Etsy?

The Internet has made marketing opportunities for crafters infinitely easier by providing venues to build online stores as an alternative to expensive brick-and-mortar stores.

Take eBay as an example. For years, a woman ran a downtown shop just over a mile from where I live and conduct my business. She specialized in antiques, collectibles, and selected craft items, particularly country crafts. I used to visit her shop every few months, but the last time I was there, the place was almost empty, and what remained was marked down for quick sale.

When I asked if she was going out of business, she said, "No, just changing my marketing ways." She went on to explain that she had started selling a few items on eBay from time to time, but the demand turned out to be great enough that she sold more there than at her shop. So she closed her shop and began working at home. Not only has she significantly increased her profits, but she's also no longer paying rent on a downtown store.

Another online marketing option is Etsy.com, designed for buying and selling handmade items. As with eBay, Etsy makes it simple to get started as a seller with easy-to-follow instructions to set yourself up in business. Many crafters have reported excellent success with Etsy stores.

Anyone interested in selling craft items on eBay.com or Etsy.com will find plenty of information on those websites. There are also a number of books in the Selected Bibliography in the back of this book that can help.

Developing New Products, Services, and Markets

Eventually, your business will probably grow to a point of saturation, either yours or the market's. When that happens, you may or may not wish to keep expanding. If you're comfortable with the size of your business and income, you can reduce your marketing effort to maintaining the status quo and replacing markets that fall by the wayside. By then your reputation might even be such that your business won't need much publicity, promotion, or advertising.

During your business's formative years, or possibly for the life of your business, you'll need to be concerned with continued growth and increased profits. If you are managing wisely and getting as much as possible out of every dollar you earn and spend, you will need to turn your attention to developing new products and markets as ways of increasing income and profits.

I've been running my own business for more than thirty years, and I still remain alert for new marketing opportunities. I keep a list of markets I haven't yet cracked but would like to. I then try to develop one or several new markets or upgrade existing ones each year.

Identify Your Opportunities

No matter what kinds of products you create and sell, you'll discover other products and services you can provide and a great number and variety of potential new markets. Before you venture into new areas, though, you need to consider carefully the kinds of work that interest you, the kinds that don't, and those that are of marginal interest. You need to identify and analyze the markets as well. And it's equally important to know and understand your limitations.

I enjoy working at several crafts, and there are a number of others that are intriguing enough for me to try my hand at. Some, however, don't interest me in the least, and others require more technical or artistic expertise than I possess. Certain crafts require only a minimal investment in tools and machinery or are compatible with the equipment I already own. Others require equipment I consider prohibitively expensive or for which I cannot justify the investment.

It's important to keep all such considerations in mind when you think about expanding your business and developing new markets.

The Show Must Go On—and On, and On, and On . . .

During tight financial times some marketing outlets go out of business, which can leave you high and dry if they represent a substantial part of your income—especially if you don't have alternative markets to fall back on.

I have learned from such experiences that I must continually strive to develop new markets and improve my existing ones, but too often I have so much work that I don't have time for that crucial part of my operation. All I can do then is promise myself I will do better when the pressure is off.

Toward that end, I make only one New Year's resolution and repeat it every January 1. I have it printed in bold black on an index card pinned to the bulletin board above my computer desk. It reads simply: WORK SMARTER THIS YEAR!

A Dozen Ways to Expand Your Craft Business

1. *Represent other artists and artisans.* If you enjoy calling on shops, galleries, and other sales outlets, consider becoming a sales rep for other arts-and-crafts professionals in your region. You can continue selling your own products and earn commissions on the works of others.

2. *Start an arts-and-crafts co-op.* Get the names and addresses of other artists and crafts professionals in your community and nearby vicinity. Schedule a meeting and invite them all to attend. Then discuss the prospects of forming a local co-op. You can then rent a building where you can set up stalls for each participating exhibitor. Members can take turns staffing the cash register. With a dozen members, your turn will come up only once every twelve business days.

3. *Organize and promote arts-and-crafts exhibits.* Meet with mall managers, city officials, and others in charge of renting building space, including community buildings and armories, and find out what it costs to rent exhibit space for a weekend. Then organize arts-and-crafts exhibits and rent space to exhibitors. You manage and advertise the event and earn a profit for your trouble.

4. *Sell your designs or patterns.* If you've come up with some popular and highly salable designs for craft items, have your designs, working plans, or patterns offset-printed. Then sell them to crafts hobbyists and other crafts professionals. You can sell them directly at craft fairs, through craft magazines, and on the Internet.

5. *Publish an artsy-craftsy newsletter.* If you own a computer and word-processing or desktop-publishing software and have some writing and editing ability, consider publishing a newsletter and selling subscriptions to hobbyists and professionals interested in crafts.

6. *Write and sell craft how-to articles.* Put your writing ability and word processor to work producing articles that describe and illustrate how to make various craft items. If you're an expert artisan but a mediocre-to-terrible writer, collaborate with a professional writer and split the profits.

7. *Write and sell craft how-to books.* If you can write and sell craft articles, you can write and sell craft books. If your ideas and designs are good enough but your writing's not, find an interested writer to collaborate with you.

8. *Sell arts-and-crafts supplies.* Find wholesale sources for the arts-and-crafts supplies that sell best to hobbyists and professionals and stock them for resale. You can sell them at craft fairs and from your home.

9. *Add related craft items to your line.* If your business has settled into a holding pattern, give it a jolt by adding related craft items to the line you now produce. You probably already have all the necessary tools on hand and many of the essential materials.

10. *Add unrelated craft items to your line.* Learning a new craft can be time-consuming, but it can also prove to be highly profitable. Unrelated craft items added to an already successful line will provide variety and broaden your market base.

11. *Start a direct-mail business.* Get busy photographing your line; then put a brochure or catalog together. Buy targeted mailing lists and bulk-mail your promotional material to prospective direct-mail buyers. Don't overlook the possibility of selling craft materials and supplies as well as finished craft items.

12. *Put your computer to work.* Your computer can help you broaden your market base and increase your profits in a variety of ways. Buy inexpensive calligraphy software and offer that service as part of your business. Buy software for horoscopes and news of the past; then take your computer on the road with you and sell horoscopes and special "this day in history" birthday and anniversary greetings at craft fairs, swap meets, and flea markets.

04 Financial Planning

In the broadest sense, the operation of any business can be divided into two basic categories: the management of money and the management of time. Although the two are inextricably intertwined, you should first expend your efforts toward planning and managing financial matters.

For most people, starting a new business involves a great deal of guess-work. I suspect that's one reason so many small businesses soon end up in financial difficulty. The home-based artisan has the distinct advantage of being able to operate part-time before starting a full-time business. The ability to analyze revenues and expenditures from the part-time business and extrapolate them to reflect full-time operation removes much of the speculation and makes the financial planning more accurate and the management much easier.

Even if you start your business on a part-time basis, however, you must not treat it as a hobby. I suspect that most artisans who decide to start a craft business began as serious amateurs who sold enough work to buy craft equipment and materials and offset the costs of their hobby. A business—part-time or full-time—must do more than that. It must generate sufficient revenue to cover expenditures *and make a profit*.

I can't stress enough the importance of being cost conscious and ever vigilant against rising expenditures. Cutting and containing costs must be a constant concern from the onset—even before you establish your business.

It's never too soon to begin planning and managing finances. If you're a hobbyist looking forward to turning your hobby into a business, begin keeping good records immediately. Learn exactly what everything costs and keep track of price increases. Conduct time studies to learn how long it takes you to do everything associated with your craft—and that includes management as well as the creative process. Then look for ways to cut costs and reduce time in all areas of your operation.

Start-Up Costs

Before launching your business, you need to estimate what it will cost you. If you have kept good records of your amateur activities, estimating start-up costs should prove much easier. Nevertheless, it will still require some guessing, albeit guessing based on experience.

Even if you've never bought a new car and know little or nothing about cars, it's easy to learn approximately what such a purchase will cost. You simply do a little research, shop around, compare various makes and models, decide which features you need and which you don't, then negotiate the best deal possible.

Some new entrepreneurs expect determining the start-up costs of implementing a new business to be just as straightforward and clear-cut. Sadly, it is not. There is no way to calculate the exact costs of running a business until you're running it, and even then you must stay alert for potential surprises.

If that sounds like a risky Catch-22, you have grasped the concept. However, you can greatly reduce the risks and improve the accuracy of your estimates by keeping good records as an amateur and then as a part-time professional.

You'll find that not all the projections, statements, and reports the accountants, consultants, and business writers insist we use are of equal value to all businesses; some are downright useless. Even those that are useful operating tools for running your business might prove to be of little or no value in the start-up process. Moreover, what works for one business or one manager might be less valuable to another. So find the tools that work for you.

In the pages that follow are some tips and tricks that should help steer you in the right direction and help you realistically estimate what the cost of starting your business might be.

Schedule of Estimated Start-Up Costs

One document you will need is a schedule of estimated start-up costs.

This is a list of all the equipment, materials, supplies, and expenses associated with running your home-based craft business. Compiling the list will force you to dwell on important details you might otherwise ignore, such as what insurance will cost, how much raw material you'll have to stock, what your phone and utilities will cost—in short, how expensive this business is going to be. The total of all these costs will be the start-up target you'll need to aim for as you plan your business.

Most of the business guides I've reviewed recommend that new entrepreneurs have at least three months' operating capital before launching a new business, and few mention anything about the owner's salary. You will certainly want to include your salary as part of any start-up projection you make. What's more, you ought to have more backing you than a mere three months' worth of funding for a full-time business.

I ran my business part-time until I had a year's salary and expenses in the bank, and all the while I was investing in and upgrading equipment. By the time I was ready to go full-time, my business was in good shape, and I was able to run it without many financial worries. I suggest you take a similar route and make sure you have at least six months' salary and operating capital backing you.

Estimated Start-Up Costs

1. Decorating and remodeling _____
2. Furniture and fixtures _____
3. Office equipment _____
4. Craft equipment _____
5. Vehicle _____
6. Insurance _____
7. Licenses and permits _____
8. Legal and professional fees _____
9. Office supplies and materials _____
10. Craft supplies and materials _____
11. Stationery and business cards _____
12. Advertising _____
13. Unexpected expenses _____
Total Estimated Start-up Costs _____

Opening Bank Accounts

I've read a number of publications that insist the first thing an entrepreneur must do is head for a bank and open a business checking account. The authors warn that you must never use a personal checking account for business purposes. One reason given is that business and personal accounts must be kept separate for bookkeeping and tax purposes. Another is that vendors and others you deal with won't think much of you if you pay with personal checks. What utter nonsense!

So what is the home-based entrepreneur with two separate accounts to do at bill-paying time? Write personal checks for the home or personal portion of the electric bill and auto insurance, then write business checks for the business portions? What a bookkeeper's nightmare that would be.

As one who has been managing some kind of business—either mine or somebody else's—for more than forty years, I can tell you that nobody is going to care one whit about being paid with a personal check instead of a business check, providing there are sufficient funds in the account. My wife and I have written more than 14,000 checks on the account we're now using. A creditor is going to worry a lot less about my personal check #14875 than business check #11 from some outfit that's been operating for about a month.

More than one publication suggests that aspiring entrepreneurs can shake the onus of the obviously new business checking account by ordering checks that begin with higher numbers. In other words, instead of a sequential check-numbering system that begins with check #1 or #101, you should direct the printer to start with #1001 and put something over on suppliers and others whose products and services you purchase. Anyone who thinks this ruse has escaped the attention of vendors and their credit managers is naive. What's more, credit managers don't set up new accounts until they've run credit investigations. So credit will be extended to you before anyone has even seen the color of your money.

If you already have a personal checking account, use it. If not, set one up. If you prefer a business checking account, that's all right too, but don't establish one for the wrong reasons.

I do recommend that you set up a separate business savings account rather than use a personal savings account for business. The extra account won't cost you anything and will make it easy to keep business funds separate. An alternative is to skip the business savings account and open an interest-bearing checking account for your business. Visit a number of banks and find out what they offer. Then establish the kind of account that provides the most and costs the least.

My wife and I had a joint checking account that I also used for business for eighteen years. I had a savings account for my business at the same bank for just as long. We also have a personal savings account at another bank. Both banks have branches less than a mile from our home, which is one of the reasons we chose them.

In 1993 we closed the checking and business savings accounts and opened new accounts at the bank where we have our personal savings account. The bank we'd done business with since 1975 kept boosting service charges and had begun charging for services that used to be free. A little gouge here, a little gouge there, and before long the accounts were costing us far more than they should. When the bank started charging me for deposit slips, I decided it was time to take our business elsewhere. The move has saved us more than $200 a year.

Don't let the cost of an account, however, be your sole guide. Consider the importance of convenience and simplicity. For example, by shopping around, you will probably discover that some banks offer lower monthly service charges than others, and a few might have no service charges at all. But you must also weigh the value of conveniences, such as proximity to your home, parking, and drive-up windows. If you save a dollar a month on service charges only to spend thirty extra minutes a week driving to and from the bank, you're wasting two hours a month and losing money in the process. Time is money in any business, and it pays to manage both wisely.

The Personal Financial Statement

Do you know what you're worth? Your creditors may want to know, and any institution you approach for a long-term loan certainly will. To answer the question, you should prepare a *personal financial statement,* also known as a *statement of financial condition,* or *statement of net worth.*

This is a relatively simple form with two columns. To prepare it, start by creating a form with your name, address, and phone number centered at the top of the page.

In the left column list all your assets: cash, checking accounts, savings accounts, real estate, stocks, bonds, securities, and accounts receivable. Also list such assets as vehicles and equipment that have cash value after allowing for depreciation. When you add up this column, you'll arrive at a figure that represents your total assets.

Name _____

Address _____

Phone_____

Assets

		## Liabilities	
Cash	_____	Accounts Payable	_____
Checking Accounts	_____	Contracts Payable	_____
Savings Accounts	_____	Notes Payable	_____
Stocks	_____	Taxes Payable	_____
Bonds	_____	Real Estate Loans	_____
Securities	_____	Vehicle Loans	_____
Real Estate	_____	Other Liabilities	_____
Vehicles	_____		
Accounts Receivable	_____		
Other Liquid Assets	_____		
Total Assets	_____	**Total Liabilities**	_____
		Net Worth	_____
		(assets minus liabilities)	

In the right column list all your liabilities: accounts payable, contracts payable, notes payable, taxes payable, real estate loans, and anything else you owe. When you add up this column, you'll arrive at a figure that represents your total liabilities.

Subtract your total liabilities from your total assets and enter the result as your net worth.

Keep this statement on hand and update it periodically—at least every year. You will probably want to include it as part of your business plan (covered in chapter 7).

Columnar Pads for Accounting and Bookkeeping

Those who prefer to conduct all or most aspects of their business on a computer will find a variety of financial-planning programs available from computer software sources. Programs designed for use by accountants and financial planners, however, generally prove to be too expensive and complex for the typical home-based business manager. Simpler, less-expensive programs, such as the popular Quicken products, are much more suitable for small business. You'll find information about the Quicken product line at www.quicken.intuit.com.

Frankly, I have found accounting and bookkeeping programs more confining and time-consuming than the manual system I have used for years. Some computer programs keep me trapped in my office, tied to my computer, far longer than I care to be. Whether you plan to keep books manually or by computer, you may want to try the system that has worked for me for decades.

Accountants usually prepare various statements on computer spreadsheets or columnar pads, the sizes of which range from 8½ by 11 inches to 14 by 17 inches and include versions with three, four, six, eight, thirteen, and fourteen columns.

Use whatever size and format of columnar pad works best for you, but be advised that the outsize, unwieldy pads are a nuisance to store.

For a number of reasons, I use one size and style of pad for all my accounting and bookkeeping: a vertical-format, four-column pad that measures 8½ by 11 inches. The format and standard letter size make such pads compatible with all my documents and files. They adapt handily to any application and fit neatly into a three-ring binder. I use them for making monthly, quarterly, annual, mid-range, and long-range studies and projections as well as for all my income-tax records. What's more, I need only stock one size, so I order a dozen fifty-sheet pads at a time, thus markedly reducing my per-pad price.

Profit-and-Loss Projections and Reports

A profit-and-loss statement (often called a P&L) is an accounting document that measures or predicts your business's operation in terms of net sales or fees, less expenses and other costs, to create an accurate profit picture or reasonable profit prediction.

By definition, this document increases in management value with the life of the business, because its degree of accuracy depends on profit history. As defined, it's of marginal value for many start-up businesses.

You can make this a useful management tool if you will follow my recommendations and forgive my nagging. Keeping accurate records of all transactions during your amateur and part-time days and logging all the hours you spend working at your craft business will create a profit history you can use to make accurate projections for your full-time business.

The columnar pad commonly recommended for P&L statements is of horizontal format, with a 3-inch-wide column on the left and thirteen narrow columns across each page. To enter both estimated and actual figures for each month and the year-end totals, you can draw a vertical line down the center of each narrow column, creating twenty-six columns in all.

In my system, I forgo the ability to scan twenty-six columns on a single page, but I gain much more in the way of readability. Instead of a single statement that reflects estimated and actual figures, I prepare two separate documents: a P&L *projection* for estimated figures, and a P&L *report* for actual figures.

You will probably find that the calendar year works best as your business's fiscal year. Unless you start your business in January, though, the first months of operation will constitute a partial year. After that, however, you can do all projecting, calculating, bookkeeping, and reporting according to the standard January-to-December calendar.

If you use four-column pads, your profit-and-loss projection for the first full year will take up four pages. On the first page, create a column each for January, February, March, and First Quarter. Subsequent pages will reflect income and expenses for the remaining months and quarters.

The second-year P&L projection will require one page, with one column devoted to each quarter. Add a line at the bottom of the page for the year-end total. Add the totals for the four columns and enter the profit or loss as the year-end total.

For the long-range P&L projection, use one page with a column each for third-year, fourth-year, and fifth-year totals.

Profit-and-Loss Projection/Report (Estimated/Actual)

	January	February	March	First Quarter Totals
REVENUE				
Services				
Merchandise sales				
Total Revenue				
COST OF GOODS SOLD				
Materials and supplies				
Outside labor				
Shipping				
Miscellaneous				
Total Cost of Goods Sold				
Gross Profit				
EXPENSES				
Wages/salaries				
Payroll deductions				
Advertising				
Vehicle				
Depreciation				
Insurance				
Interest paid				
Legal & professional fees				
Office supplies				
Rent/lease				
Repairs & maintenance				
Supplies				
Permits & licenses				
Travel & entertainment				
Utilities				
Telephone				
Postal				
Dues & publications				
Printing & copying				
Trash collection				
Miscellaneous				
Total Expenses				
Net Profit (Loss)				

In the left column of the P&L projection, under *Revenue*, list income from sale of services and merchandise on separate lines. Add the two, and enter a figure for *Total Revenue*.

Under *Cost of Goods Sold*, list amounts paid for materials and supplies, outside labor, shipping, and miscellaneous costs. Add this column, and enter a figure for *Total Cost of Goods Sold*.

Subtract *Total Cost of Goods Sold* from *Total Revenue* and enter the result as *Gross Profit*.

Under the heading of *Expenses*, list wages (including any salary you extract from the business), payroll deductions (if you have employees), and all overhead and other expenses associated with operating your business. Add this column, and enter the sum as *Total Expenses*.

Subtract *Total Expenses* from *Gross Profit* and enter the result as your projected or estimated *Net Profit (Loss)* for that accounting period.

During your first full year of business, prepare a profit-and-loss report at the end of each quarter. These reports are identical in form to the P&L projections, except that they reflect actual instead of estimated numbers. Comparing the P&L projections with the P&L reports should help you make more precise estimates in the future and more accurate mid-range and long-range projections.

Use your first-year P&L projection as your operating budget. At the end of your first full year of operation, use your P&L reports to adjust your projections and create a month-by-month projection and budget for the upcoming year.

In effect, after your first year of business, the second-year projection becomes the first year in your five-year profit-and-loss projection. That is, at the end of each year, you should create a new five-year P&L projection, following the same format as your original P&L projection.

Whatever technique you use to keep track of your expenses and income, remember these three words: documentation, documentation, documentation. You should be saving and filing all receipts, invoices, and other proof of transactions in appropriate folders. I can guarantee that extensive and detailed documentation will make your tax preparer very happy.

Balance Sheets

A balance sheet is so named because the assets listed in the left column should equal the liabilities in the right column plus the owner's equity. It's a fairly useless

[Your Business Name]

Assets		**Liabilities**	
Cash (bank accounts)		Accounts Payable	
Accounts Receivable	_____	Short-Term Notes	_____
Inventory (if applicable)	_____	Amount Due on Long-Term Notes	_____
Prepaid Expenses	_____	Interest Payable	_____
Short-Term Investments	_____	Taxes Payable	_____
		Payroll	_____
Total Current Assets	$_____	**Total Current Liabilities**	$_____
Long-Term Investments	_____		
Land	_____		
Buildings (cost)	_____		
Less Depreciation	_____		
Net Value	$_____	**Owner's Equity**	$_____
Equipment (cost)	_____	(assets minus liabilities)	
Less Depreciation	_____		
Net Value	$_____		
Furniture/Fixtures (cost)	_____		
Less Depreciation	_____		
Net Value	$_____	**Total Liabilities & Equity**	$_____
Vehicles (cost)	_____		
Less Depreciation	_____		
Net Value	$_____	Current Date_____
Total Fixed Assets	$_____		
Other Assets	$_____		
Total Assets	$_____		

document for new businesses and may be of only marginal value for many sole proprietors. (See chapter 6 for a definition of *sole proprietor*.) Of all the analytical and forecasting documents, I have found the balance sheet the least useful and informative for my home-based business. It might prove useful, however, if you need to seek financing, so you should know what it is and how to create one.

Balance sheets are usually prepared at the end of the year. The so-called *pro forma balance sheet* is one prepared in advance of the coming year or accounting period and is hypothetical in nature.

Cash-Flow Projections and Reports

Cash flow is more than net profit; it's how money moves into and out of a business. It covers all business income and cash reserves after expenditures and can indicate the timing of cash movement.

For your business to succeed, it's essential that you ensure a steady and substantial income, not only to pay business expenses and to buy materials and equipment, but also to provide you with an adequate personal income and benefits.

You must keep track of cash flow by regular reporting of income and expenditures. In most businesses, this is done monthly, with quarterly and yearly totals included. Accurate and timely records will enable you to track cash flow and forecast future needs and trends, which in turn will allow you to make intelligent capital investments and ward off potential problems or interruptions of cash flow.

Cash-flow projections and reports are similar in form and format to profit-and-loss projections and reports. In fact, they're similar in content, but with two important exceptions. Profit-and-loss projections and reports are designed to provide estimated and actual net profits before taxes, and they do not include cash-reserve information. Cash-flow projections and reports provide estimated and actual after-tax profits plus available cash reserves to indicate a cash position at the end of an accounting period: month, quarter, or year.

To prepare a cash-flow projection for one year, you can use a sheet from a thirteen-column pad or four sheets from a four-column pad as I do. As with the P&L projections and reports, each four-column page provides a column each for three months and one column for quarter totals.

In the left column, Item 1 should be *Cash on Hand* as of the first of the month. This includes any currency earmarked for business purposes as well as amounts in any business bank accounts.

Item 2 is *Cash Receipts* for the month—itemized as cash sales, collected receivables, and any other receipts, including any cash infusion—from your business savings, the sale of capital equipment, or any other source.

Item 3 is *Total Cash Receipts*. Add Item 1 and Item 3 and enter that figure as Item 4: *Total Cash Available*.

Item 5 is *Cash Expenditures*. Under that heading, itemize and list all cash that your business had to pay out during that accounting period, including all wages (yours and any others'), all taxes, all expenses, and all overhead. You can modify this listing to suit your needs. In my own cash-flow projection, I have itemized subheads alphabetically, from *a* to *v*.

Item 6 is *Total Cash Paid*: the sum of everything listed under *Cash Expenditures*. Subtract Item 6 from Item 4 and enter the result as Item 7: *Cash Position*.

At the end of any accounting period, when *Total Cash Available* is greater than *Total Cash Paid*, a positive figure will represent your *Cash Position*. If *Total Cash Paid* is greater than *Total Cash Available*, your *Cash Position* will be a negative figure, also referred to as *negative cash flow*.

The purpose of the cash-flow projection is to identify any negative cash position so that you can take action to rectify the situation.

As with the profit-and-loss documents, you should also prepare a cash-flow report, which is identical to the cash-flow projection except that it reflects actual instead of estimated figures. Regularly comparing the two documents will help you become more accurate in your forecasting.

I know that, barring any unforeseen catastrophe, my most troublesome months will be June and December. They have been for more than fifteen years and probably will continue to be. For quite a few years, November has been my third most expensive month and May has come up a close fourth.

Not only can I predict which months might slip into a negative cash position, but I also know why. In June and December, in addition to all the usual expenses, I have several hefty semiannual and annual bills to pay—mainly insurance premiums. Also, spring and fall are my busiest seasons, so I'm on the road a good bit then. I always charge my fuel and motel bills to credit cards. This is also a time when I must constantly replenish supplies. It can take from thirty to sixty days for all these charges to show up on my credit card bills. Those arriving earliest are usually due in May and November, but the bulk of them end up in my accounts-payable file in June and December.

Cash-Flow Projection/Report (Estimated/Actual)

	January	February	March	First Quarter Totals
1. Cash on Hand				
(1st of month)	_____	_____	_____	_____
2. Cash Receipts				
a. Cash Sales	_____	_____	_____	_____
b. Collected Receivables	_____	_____	_____	_____
c. Other	_____	_____	_____	_____
3. Total Cash Receipts	_____	_____	_____	_____
4. Total Cash Available	_____	_____	_____	_____
5. Cash Expenditures	_____	_____	_____	_____
a. Gross Wages	_____	_____	_____	_____
b. Taxes	_____	_____	_____	_____
c. Materials	_____	_____	_____	_____
d. Supplies (office, etc.)	_____	_____	_____	_____
e. Services	_____	_____	_____	_____
f. Repairs & Maintenance	_____	_____	_____	_____
g. Advertising	_____	_____	_____	_____
h. Vehicle	_____	_____	_____	_____
i. Travel & Entertainment	_____	_____	_____	_____
j. Accounting & Legal	_____	_____	_____	_____
k. Rent	_____	_____	_____	_____
l. Telephone	_____	_____	_____	_____
m. Utilities	_____	_____	_____	_____
n. Insurance	_____	_____	_____	_____
o. Printing & Copying	_____	_____	_____	_____
p. Postage	_____	_____	_____	_____
q. UPS, FedEx, etc.	_____	_____	_____	_____
r. Dues & Publications	_____	_____	_____	_____
s. Miscellaneous	_____	_____	_____	_____
t. Other	_____	_____	_____	_____
u. Subtotal	_____	_____	_____	_____
v. Capital Expenditures	_____	_____	_____	_____
6. Total Cash Paid (u plus v)	_____	_____	_____	_____
7. Cash Position (4 minus 6)	_____	_____	_____	_____

Twenty years ago I couldn't have made such predictions. But by preparing certain useful projections and reports and paying attention to how cash moves through my business, I can now do a pretty good job of forecasting trends. Consequently, I'm able to use these figures to my best advantage—whether to tighten my purse strings to see my business through some lean days or make a timely capital investment.

Cash-flow analysis can be much more complicated, and usually is, for larger, more complex businesses. Sadly, some writers, consultants, and educators insist the topic be just as cumbersome and confusing for owners of small businesses. They tend to make it an academic exercise that serves little practical purpose for the home-based entrepreneur. My advice is this: Try to keep it as simple as possible.

Credit and Borrowing

Although many entrepreneurs start businesses on borrowed capital, I don't recommend this practice. Instead of borrowing start-up cash, you stand a much better chance of succeeding if you work part-time, invest in equipment, and build a substantial savings account before launching a full-time business. Don't start with long-term debt.

Credit Cards and Vendor Accounts

Short-term debt is another matter, and it takes many shapes. Every time you pay for a tank of gas with an oil company credit card, you aren't really paying for it; you're putting off payment until the company sends you a bill. Likewise with the motel bill you put on an American Express card, the computer software you charge to a Visa account, or the tool purchase you put on a MasterCard. When you charge office and craft supplies and materials to accounts you have established with vendors, you also take on short-term debt.

This form of borrowing is not only an acceptable practice, but it also can offer a number of advantages when properly managed. Credit cards and vendor accounts can be a great aid to bookkeeping. They eliminate the need to keep large amounts of cash on hand, and they reduce the number of checks you must write.

They also speed up delivery of mail orders, because your supplier can ship immediately instead of waiting for a check to clear. If you run into a problem with a supplier, you stand a better chance of getting quick satisfaction if you charged your order to a major credit card, because the credit card company will contact the supplier on your behalf. This not only saves you time and trouble, but it also exerts more pressure on the supplier than you could ever hope to.

Along with the advantages of credit cards, be aware of the dangers. As a new start-up business, you may be tempted to charge too much on credit cards and then be unable to pay them off in full each month. This will trap you into long-term, high-interest debt. A great deal of the personal financial woes of today's economic climate can be laid squarely at the feet of peoples' love affair with credit cards.

If—and that's a big *if*—you pay off your bill every month, only then should you consider the judicious use of a credit card. A paid-in-full credit card can also increase your credit rating.

Credit Card Traps

Along with the notoriously and unnecessarily high interest rates that most credit card issuers charge are other costs you should be aware of and should try to avoid. Some of the features and services that credit card companies offer might sound great but prove to be only marginally valuable or utterly useless. Moreover, some companies use ploys to attract potential cardholders by playing on their egos.

Whenever you consider signing up for a credit card, look for a company that charges little or nothing in the way of annual fees. If any annual fee exceeds $25, go elsewhere, or make sure the company offers useful features and incentives that make such a fee worth paying.

At one time, major credit card companies charged no annual fee and no interest on new purchases for about the first thirty days. Instead, they made their profits from the interest they charged on revolving credit. Now many companies not only are charging annual fees but also have eliminated the grace period on new purchases, thus earning interest on all purchases from the moment they're charged to the account. Try to find companies that allow a grace period of twenty-five to thirty days on all new purchases; then pay off your accounts as they come due. This way you will be able to make interest-free credit purchases and build an outstanding credit record in the process.

Some credit card companies that charge exorbitant annual fees and high interest rates try to attract business by offering cardholders incentives, ranging from discounts on car rentals and lodging to travel club benefits and annual financial reports. Make sure that any such features will be of real value to you and your business.

Several of my credit cards and memberships in professional associations entitle me to 10 percent discounts on car rentals at specific agencies. These discounts, however, are usually disallowed on special low-cost rental packages. By shopping around for the best deal, I have always beaten the paltry 10 percent discount—a worthless feature for me that probably will be for you as well.

I travel a good bit, so when a company offered me its highly touted Corporate Card, with discounts of 20 to 50 percent on hotel rooms, I jumped at the chance. I thought I could save a bundle, so the $75 annual fee didn't bother me. What I later learned, however, was that few of the hotel chains on the small list of cooperating establishments had facilities in the cities I visit. I canceled the card before paying the annual fee.

I also canceled one gold card when it became obvious that I was paying $75 a year simply for the color gold. None of the other card privileges was of any value to me. A colleague of mine canceled his $300-a-year platinum card for similar reasons.

Credit card marketing people will try to inflate your ego by telling you how important you'll be when you carry their gold or platinum card. In reality, however, nobody gives a hoot about the color of your card. As long as accounts are in good standing and charges have not exceeded credit limits, in vendors' eyes, all cards are the color of greenbacks.

Credit card companies make it temptingly easy to get into debt. Just think of all the frequent flier miles you could accrue if you purchased all your supplies with a credit card! But unless you are disciplined enough to pay off that credit card in full every month, this is too simple (and deep) a trap to fall into.

For the small home craft business, it is a far safer and more intelligent proposition to keep your business transactions clean and simple. Don't think it's safe to load up a credit card with debt in order to fund your start-up costs, because if the business fails, you're still in debt.

Debit Cards

Many banks issue debit cards, which resemble credit cards only in appearance. Purchases made by debit card are paid for out of your bank account and are usually charged to the user's account immediately.

A debit card can be an excellent alternative to a credit card because you are never tempted to spend beyond your means. Starting in 2000, bank regulations on debit cards improved to the point where there is just as much protection offered for debit cards as there is for credit cards in cases of theft and fraud.

While all sorts of "freebies" and benefits are dangled in front of you for using a credit card, the fact is banks prefer to suck you into revolving debt from which you may never escape, and statistics indicate that 60 percent of all credit card users do not pay off their credit cards in full each month.

One of the biggest reasons new businesses fail is due to poor business practices—and this includes acquiring debt. If you want to give your craft business the maximum potential to succeed, it may be safer to use a debit card instead.

For those who are concerned that a thief can empty your bank account with a stolen debit card, it's a simple matter to open a separate checking account dedicated to debit card use. This way thieves are incapable of wiping out more than you have in that particular account. Coupled with bank liability protection, a debit card is a very safe option.

And, just as important, you are not tempted to spend beyond your immediate ability to pay. The one thing a debit card will never do is get you into debt.

Debit cards can be "opted in" or "opted out" of overdraft amounts. When "opted in," you are telling the bank to allow you to make a purchase in excess of the amount currently in your debit account. The bank will accept the purchase, but charge you an overdraft fee, usually $30.

When "opted out," you cannot go over your available funds and the debit card will be declined at the point of sale. (I find this to be a safer—and cheaper—option.)

Overdraft protection is also available for debit cards. In these cases, the bank will pull funds from another authorized account and transfer those funds to your debit card, at no fee.

There are occasional limitations on the use of debit cards. Some rental car companies, hotels, or airlines do not accept debit cards. It is your responsibility to check in advance to confirm what form of payment these companies accept. If they don't take debit cards, consider using a different company.

Long-Term Debt

Even if you adopt a policy of avoiding long-term debt, sooner or later you will probably have to borrow for your business. For example, you may have to replace an expensive piece of equipment, upgrade a computer system, or buy a new vehicle. It's not always possible to make such high-ticket purchases without a long-term loan.

You might also land contracts that force you to borrow for capital investment. For example, doing the best and most cost-effective job might hinge on your owning certain equipment. Or it could be that just as you are trying to get a few more months' use out of your vehicle, your business suddenly begins demanding considerable travel. These are times when borrowing now could pay off handsomely later.

Under such circumstances, be sure to shop around for the best interest rates. Before you visit bankers, head for your local Small Business Development Center or write to the U.S. Small Business Administration for information about its loan programs, such as the guaranteed loan program, export revolving line of credit, and small loan program. The SBDC can alert you to any other state and federal programs for which you might qualify. Among the most common are special loans for veterans, women, and members of minority groups.

Know What's on Your Credit Report

Everybody in America who has a credit history is in the computer files of at least one credit-reporting company. You can obtain your credit report by phone, by mail (in a request to the credit reporting bureau), or online. You are allowed one free credit report each year from each of the three credit reporting agencies: Equifax (www.equifax.com), Experian (www.experian.com), and TransUnion (www.transunion.com). To obtain your free annual credit report, visit www.annualcreditreport.com, which partners with the federal government to provide credit scores.

Many people have complained about errors in their credit reports, which have caused them trouble when applying for loans. You need to examine your own credit report to determine your credit rating and the accuracy of the information in the report. If you find errors, get them corrected immediately; they can affect your credit rating and interfere with your ability to secure financing.

One of the most important and difficult questions that faces every aspiring home-based entrepreneur is, "How much should I charge for my products or services?" I have no pat answers or useful formulas to help you with this question because there are too many variables to consider. I can no more tell you what to charge your customers than a bed-and-breakfast innkeeper in Fargo can tell a San Diego hotel owner how to set rates. Both might be in the lodging business, but beyond that, there are simply too many differences.

Local cost of living is a major determinant. It's far cheaper to live and do business in North Dakota than in California. Even one part of a state can differ greatly from another. In northern California, for example, you can still find a clean, comfortable, modern motel room for less than $55 a night; in southern California, I've seen RV spaces go for that much.

Every business is different. One artisan might specialize in beadwork while another works exclusively as a potter. In a more diversified business, one individual may make and sell toys, puzzles, games, and a variety of country crafts. Some peddle their wares directly to local gift and specialty shops, whereas others prefer to handle only the creative side of the business and let a representative or agent take care of sales. An artisan in New York, Los Angeles, or Seattle may have to gross $600 a day to make a living; one based in rural mid-America might get by on $300 a day in sales and live just as comfortably.

Only you can determine what to charge for your craft products and talents, so you will have to do your homework. Although some books and associations can help, in the end your pricing policy will be based on what crafts you produce, how you operate, how you stack up against the competition, where you sell your work, and where you do your work.

No matter what craft constitutes your main business interest, you'll have your work cut out for you in the initial pricing process. You will also find that you must constantly monitor costs and competition so that you will know when and how much to increase prices.

Don't fret. Expect some difficulty in the beginning, and be assured that you'll learn from trial and error. You'll probably make some mistakes, as most of us do. You'll know you've overpriced some items when they don't sell well. And you'll kick yourself when a new product line sells out immediately because you've underpriced it. You'll know better next time. Take comfort in the fact that pricing and price monitoring become much easier over the long haul.

As in any craft business, your prices will depend mainly on the cost of running your business (overhead), the cost of materials, the value of your time, and the pricing structure of the marketplace (what the market will bear).

Fiscal Conservatism

If new business operators have a common fault, it's their overly optimistic view of how their businesses will fare. For that reason, it's best to adopt a conservative outlook and tightfisted management policy.

Don't go into business thinking you'll get rich. Plan instead to work hard for an adequate living. If you eventually get rich, good for you. Won't that be a pleasant surprise?

It's too easy to look at successful crafters and assume they've always been successful. But success takes business smarts, sound fiscal planning, and time. And never forget the far greater number of crafters you *can't* see, because they're no longer in business.

There's nothing wrong with going into business with high expectations for success. But temper those expectations with a huge dose of realism. Your product is in competition with every other booth at the craft fair, with every other web page on the Internet, with every other business out there vying for the dollar in the customer's pocket. It's up to you to garner the patience to keep improving your product, your pricing, your exposure, your market, your wholesalers, or whatever other means you can utilize to increase business. And this all takes *time*.

While you're building your business, a key component is to stay out of debt. This can mean advanced planning, such as saving now for the tool you know you'll need to replace next year. It can mean avoiding running up credit card debt in the touching hope that you'll be bringing in enough money next month to pay that bill in full. And it can mean not spending money on things you don't need.

Pricing for Profit

Before establishing prices, you will have to determine what kinds of crafts you will be creating and selling, then research those areas to determine how payment is commonly made and what it amounts to. If you plan to operate a ceramics studio, find out what other ceramists in your community or region are charging. This will provide a basis for your pricing structure—a figure to work with. Then determine how you fit into the community of local or regional ceramists.

You don't want to start out as the most expensive ceramist in town; nor should you be the cheapest. If your products are top quality and your pricing is mid-range, you can gradually increase prices as your reputation for quality and reliability grows. Even if you can work considerably cheaper than other artisans in your locale, under-cutting their prices could work against you in several ways. First, your low prices will turn away some potential customers who reason that you get what you pay for. What's more, they might invite your competitors to retaliate.

In my diversified business, income derives from many sources, including royalties, day rates, hourly jobs, flat fees, and consignments as well as wholesale and retail sales. Obviously, I've had to spend considerable time analyzing my costs and factoring in my labor and profit margins to know what I need to make. Then I've had to make adjustments according to market trends and pressures. You'll have to do the same.

Direct Costs

The direct costs associated with the manufacture of any craft include money spent for raw materials and finishing products as well as for any directly related services.

For example, a clock maker who produces wall clocks from maple burl slabs might cut his own slabs from raw burls, have them cut at a mill, or buy ready-cut slabs. If he buys the burls and cuts them himself, what he pays for the burls is a direct material cost. The work he does to cut and prepare the burls is labor, which is another, albeit important, part of the equation.

If the clock maker buys the burls and has them cut into slabs at a mill, the burls are a direct material cost, to which the mill charges can be added as a direct expense.

If he buys ready-cut burls, they are considered raw material, and what he pays is considered a direct cost.

Prices charged for clockworks, hanging hardware, and polyurethane varnish are also direct material costs. If he has a local wood shop finish-sand the slabs and an artist paint scenes on the sanded slabs, those are direct expenses.

All these direct costs constitute one part of the formula for determining what to charge for the finished clocks. What the clock maker pays to heat and light his shop, however, are indirect costs, which are treated separately in arriving at the total cost of manufacture.

Indirect Costs/Overhead

In determining what it costs to manufacture any item, you also must include the indirect costs, known as overhead. These costs include rent, utilities, office supplies, depreciation, and anything else that's not a direct material or labor cost. Most of the methods of calculating overhead when pricing a product are complicated and time-consuming and are of marginal value for most home-based craft professionals.

One fairly simple way to factor overhead into the pricing scheme is to determine indirect costs, then calculate an hourly rate for them. This method works fine for service-oriented businesses, where hourly rates tend to be high, but not so well for product-oriented craft businesses.

The only sure way to determine per-item overhead is to do careful time-and-cost studies that, in a small business, simply devour too much valuable time for what they're worth. Most of us resort to formulas that aren't much better than guesses but take far less time and work out all right in the end.

In one formula we're advised to consider indirect costs to be the equivalent of one-third of the direct costs. In other words, Direct Costs x 33.3 percent = Overhead.

A variation on the one-third theme suggests treating overhead as equivalent to one-third the cost of materials or one-third the cost of labor, whichever is greater.

"Ya pays your money, and ya takes your pick."

Labor

You must factor all labor, including your own, into the pricing equation. Labor is worth money, and it is one of the costs of manufacture.

If you're doing all the work, include your labor as part of the price of any craft object, but avoid the temptation of overpricing your labor. As the owner/manager of a successful business, perhaps your time is worth $30, $40, or more an hour, but you can't consider time spent cutting, assembling, and finishing parts of a craft object to be worth that much. When you're managing, you're worth a manager's salary; when you're laboring, you should collect a laborer's wages.

To determine how much value to assign to labor, simply find out what it would cost in your locale to hire others to perform identical or similar tasks. If you could hire someone for $10 an hour, consider your labor worth $10 an hour when you do the same job.

Profit

Profit is another important part of the pricing equation, but oddly enough it's something too many artisans ignore or confuse with labor costs. Profit and labor costs are not the same. As regards product pricing, labor—including *your* labor—is part of the cost of manufacturing the product. Profit is the company's share: what's left after all other costs.

Profit is what will allow you to expand your business, to invest in it. It's the money that will make you more money. It's the reward for your managing skills. It's the payback for the risks you take, for the extra hours you put in, for the initiative you show, for the responsibility you dare not shirk. It's what operating your own business is all about.

A friend of mine is a craftsman, and a good one. His major problem is that he doesn't consider his time very valuable. He says he has to make $100 a day to survive. If he meant $100 in profit, over and above his cost of manufacturing, that would be okay. If he were talking about $100 a day for labor, in addition to whatever profit he might make, that might be all right too. But he means he's satisfied making $100 total, after the cost of materials and overhead, and he doesn't have a good grasp of what his overhead amounts to. Twenty to thirty years ago, his $100 a day would have been good money, but not today.

In my business, I say that to spend a dollar I have to make two. When the year-end tallies are in, it usually ends up that way. Some years it's a little better, some years a little worse. Certain aspects of my business are better, or more profitable, than others.

What my friend fails to realize when he looks at that $100, literally or figuratively, at the end of a workday, is that he's not really looking at $100. By the time all the federal, state, and county taxing agencies finish with him, 40 percent of that $100 will be gone. Another 10 percent will just disappear incidentally, leaving him with about $50 to show for his day's efforts. For his usual ten-hour day, his take-home pay is about five bucks an hour, and there's no additional profit to plow back into the business. Fifty hours a week, fifty weeks a year—after expenses, taxes, and incidentals—works out to $12,500. And he wonders why he just can't seem to get ahead.

Again, profit is in addition to, over and above, above and beyond, everything else. If your business isn't making a profit, your business isn't succeeding.

So how do you determine what your profit should be? It's easy—just a loose translation of the old Golden Rule: Do to others as others do to you. If you sell craft items to gift shops for resale, to arrive at their selling prices, the shop owners simply double your price, or mark up 100 percent. If you sell an item for $10, the shop sells it for $20, or probably $19.95. If you sell an item for $100, its new price tag will probably read $199.95.

Figure your business's profit the same way. Add all the costs of manufacture and multiply that times 100 percent to determine your profit. Then add profit to the equation to arrive at the price.

Pricing Equation

Here's the simple pricing equation:

Materials + Overhead + Labor + Profit = Price

It's easy to arrive at a price for any item, providing you have kept good records. Let's assume you're making a product that takes two hours per unit and that labor costs are $10 an hour. We'll further assume that your materials and any directly related services amount to $8.50 per unit. With that small amount of information, and using the second variation of the one-third formula for calculating overhead, make the following list and calculations to determine the price to charge for each unit:

- Labor = $10/hour
- Time per unit = 2 hours = $20
- Materials per unit = $8.50
- Overhead = $20 x 33.3 percent = $6.66
- Cost of manufacture = $35.16
- Profit = $35.16 x 100 percent = $35.16
- Price per unit = $70.32 (wholesale)

If you're selling this product wholesale for $70, the retailer will mark up 100 percent and charge his customers $139.95. This equation works as well for a $10 item as for a $1,000 item.

Psychological Pricing Schemes

Any observant buyer knows there are a number of pricing schemes in use that fool some buyers into believing they're getting more for their money or are paying less than they actually are.

"Twofers" are popular in supermarkets and some discount stores. A canned product, for example, will sell better when marked two for a dollar than when marked 50 cents or even 49 cents each. Any item will sell much better priced at $1.99 or $4.98 than at $2.00 or $5.00, respectively.

At craft fairs, flea markets, swap meets, and other public sales, you might find it a nuisance to fool with pennies. So price your $10 items at $9.95, $20 items at $19.95, and $50 items at $49.95.

You can eliminate the pennies, nickels, and dimes and carry only paper money and a couple of rolls of quarters by pricing amounts under a dollar in twenty-five-cent denominations: $9.75, $18.75, $22.50, $49.50, and so on.

Reducing Costs to Increase Profits

The cost of everything that goes into your craft products—materials, supplies, overhead, and labor—affects profit. Your costs must be factored into the prices you charge your customers. Excessive costs can make your prices too high to compete effectively. One result is that you could price yourself out of business.

Consequently, you must remain ever alert for ways to reduce costs and thereby keep your profits up. You also must track your costs to know how to accommodate them in your pricing structure. Macro cost analysis is a continuing process in any well-run business, and the best tools for this job are your profit-and-loss projections and reports.

Micro cost analysis is equally important, and for this you will need to keep accurate cost-and-time studies on every product in your line. It's also a good idea to review your products regularly to look for ways of reducing costs, thereby increasing profits. You'll need to study your manufacturing processes as well as your time-and-cost records to see if there are ways you can make profitable improvements.

Managing Accounts Payable

Bills that come due regularly or irregularly are known as accounts payable. There's more to managing this crucial part of your business than simply writing checks and mailing them. You should do so in a timely fashion, and you must understand the difference between timely and on time.

If you merely stack up all your bills and write checks until you have no more money, you aren't managing well. Although most of your bills are probably payable in thirty days, some vendors offer discounts for payment submitted early in the month—usually something in the range of 1 to 5 percent if paid by the tenth of the month, then net after that. Some vendors make their bills payable in thirty days with no discount option. A typical monthly statement might show "Terms: 2 percent 10 days—Net 30." That means you have ten days from the date of the statement to deduct 2 percent from your bill; after that you must pay the full amount and must do so within one month.

Some suppliers don't send monthly statements but instead expect you to pay off the invoice. You might be allowed a total of thirty days to pay, or until the thirtieth of the month following the invoice date. If the supplier offers an early payment discount, the invoice might say something like "Terms: 3 percent 10th proximo—net 30th," which means you may take a 3 percent discount if you pay by the tenth of the month following the invoice date.

Timely Payments

If your checking account is fat, you can just pay all your bills at one sitting, but for most of us, checks and bills arrive throughout the month. Often a checking account balance might make it through only a portion of the bills and need to await the arrival and deposit of the next batch of receivables.

In such circumstances, sort all your bills into stacks, including those offering discounts for early payment, those offering no discounts, and those offering no discounts and charging late payment penalties. Obviously, the bills to pay first are the discounted ones. I have several vendors who offer 10 percent discounts and one that offers 20 percent; they get paid first every month. Next, pay those that will penalize you for late payment. That way, if you have a slight interruption of cash flow toward the end of the month, you won't have to miss paying a bill that carries a penalty with it.

When the Buck Stops Short

If you continually come up short at the end of the month, you must make some adjustments in your cash management practices. You should strive to get all your bills paid on time and in a timely way, but when the buck stops short, you need to take action.

Occasionally letting an outstanding balance slip into the thirty-day past-due category is no big deal and will have little or no effect on your credit rating. Balances that go to sixty days are more serious, and ninety days will have your creditors worrying about you.

If you run into a cash-flow problem, the first thing to do is to try to inject cash into your business to rectify it. If that's impossible, or if it might cause more serious problems elsewhere, don't just ignore your bills.

Immediately write to your creditors to explain the circumstances, assure them that this is a temporary situation that you will correct soon, and provide a date they can count on for full payment.

I ended up in such a position several years ago after I had placed large orders for materials and office supplies, counting on a substantial check due to be sent to me. When the check didn't arrive as promised, several of my payables were put in jeopardy.

I had charged the materials to a credit card, so I made the minimum payment due and let the balance slip into the high-interest revolving-credit category. I had charged the office supplies to my account with the vendor, to whom I wrote a letter and assured full payment within forty-five days. Three weeks later, the tardy check arrived, and I paid my bill and added a 2 percent late charge. Two weeks later I got a letter from the vendor thanking me for the payment and a check refunding the late charge.

Such timely and professional action will leave your credit rating intact and might even improve it. Show your business associates that you're a reliable professional, and you'll be treated like one.

Managing Accounts Receivable

Everything owed to you falls into the category of *accounts receivable*, often just called *receivables*. Managing receivables is one of the most important aspects of controlling your business's finances.

It is important to understand the difference between selling wholesale and selling retail. Very simply, who sells your product directly to the consumer? Is it you, or is it someone else?

If you sell your products directly to the end user, whether through eBay, a website, craft shows, or in a storefront, then you sell retail.

If you sell your products to a middleman who then sells them to the consumer, then you sell wholesale.

It's entirely possible to do both, of course. And dipping your toes into both wholesale and retail sales can make for a balanced and healthier business.

Get the Cash When You Can

Cash is always best; take it when you can get it. It's impossible, however, to run a craft business without getting involved in credit in one way or another. Whenever you agree to sell your products and get paid later, you are extending credit. That means credit management is a crucial part of your business.

Merchant Service Accounts

Frequently, start-up crafters think they're too small to have a merchant services account (the ability to accept credit cards). This is incorrect. Many small crafters have flourishing merchant services accounts. And the fact is, customers often prefer to pay by credit card for a number of reasons, including convenience and cardholder protection. If you as a vendor don't have the ability to accept credit cards, you stand the possibility of losing an enormous chunk of business.

If you choose to open a merchant services account, go to a reputable bank or financial institution. Sometimes crafters are approached at craft shows by dubious merchant services salespeople "fishing" for new accounts. Possibly these types of salespeople are operating under the impression that small crafters feel too intimidated to approach a larger financial institution, so they step in to fill this void. While they *may* be reputable, then again they may not. Go to a bank.

That said, you may have to wait a couple of years until you have a solid business history (assuming you have a good financial record yourself) before a bank will consider you. Ask your neighboring crafters about which financial institutions supply their merchant services account. A little research can save you money—and hassle.

Recognize that you must generally pay about 3 percent of your credit card sales as fees for the merchant services account. However, paying 3 percent of your hard-earned money to the credit card companies is better than paying nothing at all because you lost so many potential sales.

With any retail sale, even one using a credit card, give a receipt. Consider purchasing several receipt books with carbon or carbonless copies, and give a receipt for *every* transaction you make.

Take good care of any credit card slips in your possession. Shred or burn carbon copies. It is your responsibility to make sure any credit card numbers entrusted to you for purposes of a transaction don't fall into outside hands.

Retail Sales

Whenever you sell your product directly to the consumer, you will be handling money in its many forms. This is a surprisingly complex subject.

Cash

You probably won't handle a lot of cash in your day-to-day business transactions unless you're at a craft show or other direct selling venue. In these situations, you'll want to be as organized—and safe—as possible.

Start with a lockable cashbox, available at most office supply stores. Ideally it will have slots for different denominations of bills and coins, but it's also an ideal place to tuck other miscellaneous necessities—credit card slips, receipt books, a calculator, pens (at least five!—they tend to walk away on their own), safety pins, business cards, etc.

Be sure to have coins among your start-up cash, because even if your products are priced evenly on the dollar (i.e., $7, $20, $32, etc.) you will need to charge sales tax for your state. Keep a small calculator in your cash box to assist in making tallies.

The $20 bill is the commonly used bill, so have lots of $10, $5, and $1 bills to make change. There is nothing more annoying to your neighboring vendors than your having to ask them repeatedly if they can break a $20. Be prepared.

When selling an item for cash, make sure you give the customer a receipt. This acts as proof of purchase as well as contact information for you should the customer wish to purchase another item later on. You can purchase inexpensive receipt books at an office supply store.

Checks

Some new crafters are reluctant to accept checks from customers because they feel the risk of a bounced check is too high.

Certainly there is a risk, but most crafters experience minimal troubles with bounced checks. In the end, it's up to you whether or not to accept checks.

If you do accept checks, take precautions. If the customer acts shifty and nervous, then you have the option to say you prefer cash or a credit card. If you do accept a check, write down the driver's license number or at least confirm the customer's phone number and address. If your customer has no identification and refuses to give you a phone number, there is a chance he's trying to pass a bad check.

Credit Cards

Ironically, there can be more dishonesty with credit card purchases than with check purchases.

Part of the problem with "bounced" credit cards is situations when you cannot run the credit card right away and instead must depend on a manual imprinter, sometimes called a "chunk chunk" or "knucklebuster" machine. This is because you cannot determine immediately whether the customer has exceeded his credit limit.

If you have electricity but no phone line, you can rent or buy a credit card machine that will record the credit card purchase, and then everything can be downloaded at a later time as a batch file. Your merchant services rep can help you select a suitable machine for your needs. While you can't catch a maxed-out credit card on the spot, this type of machine will at least weed out many customers who know perfectly well they're maxed out (or who have a hot card) because they're fooled into thinking the machine is checking their records.

The riskiest scenario is when you have no electricity or phone line and must use a manual "chunk chunk" machine. Then you must write out the credit card slip by hand (hint: *always* get their phone number on the slip next to their signature and *don't* forget to return their credit card) and have no way of knowing whether the customer has exceeded his credit limit or has a hot card.

Despite these risks, a merchant services account is a tremendous help to the small crafter, since most customers prefer to conduct credit transactions. However, if you can't electronically verify the card at the time of sale, there is an increased risk that a customer's credit card will bounce later when you try to run it.

Needless to say, *all* cash, credit card slips, and checks should be removed from a craft show after closing. Nothing should be left in your booth, no matter how adequate the security.

Wholesale Sales

Whenever you sell your product to a middleman who then sells it to the consumer, you are involved with wholesale sales. Wholesale sales are different from retail in that you receive less per piece, but sell in greater quantity. It has the added advantage that you don't need to physically be where the consumer purchases your craft—you can stay in your shop and keep working while someone else sells your wares.

Billing Practices for Wholesale

Your first step toward managing receivables for wholesale sales is to establish systematic billing practices. For most of us, that means stocking and using invoice forms and monthly statement forms.

You will be billing only wholesale customers, since retail customers (such as those who buy your products at a craft show) will pay for your items up front. But unless your wholesale customers are in the habit of paying for the order in advance (a highly recommended procedure), then you will be regularly issuing bills for the amount owed you.

You can pick up bill forms that best suit your business and have them imprinted with your name, address, and phone number. An alternative is to use a computer to design and generate your own forms. Most word-processing software will facilitate form printing, or you can use any of a number of small-business and form-making programs. Some companies offer multipart, preprinted forms and dedicated software to streamline the billing process.

You must adopt a billing policy and use it consistently. You can use invoices and monthly statements or invoices alone. In the latter case, ask your clients or customers to pay the invoice and include instructions to that effect on the invoice: *This is the only bill you will receive. Please pay the amount due.*

I use invoices and statements because the statement often serves as a low-key, impersonal dun on accounts that slip into the thirty-days-past category. So I bill each sale with an invoice; then at month's end I send a statement to each customer with an outstanding balance. I spell out all details of the transaction on the invoice. On the subsequent statement I need only reference each unpaid invoice by number and show the amount due.

Late Charges and Follow-Up

This important message appears at the bottom of every invoice and statement: *2 percent per month (24 percent APR) applied to the balance of all accounts after 30 days*. Accounts that go past thirty days get a 2 percent charge added to the balance. After sixty days I also use a bold, red Past Due stamp on the statement.

Every account ninety days past due gets the same treatment as the sixty-day account, plus a letter from me insisting on immediate payment. If the account goes to 120 days, I send a demand letter by certified mail, insisting on payment within ten days. The next step is a phone call to my attorney for a ten-day demand letter on his letterhead.

The lawyer's demand letter works nearly every time, but that one letter costs me $50, so I don't use it for small amounts.

If all those measures fail, I'm faced with the decision to turn the account over to a collection agency or to sue. I have faced such circumstances only twice. In one instance, I decided the likelihood of collection was slim, and the amount wasn't worth the time and trouble, so I wrote it off. In the other case the amount was worth going after, but even though I was skeptical about the client's promise to pay, I agreed to let her postpone payment for six more months. Three months later her attorney sent me notice of bankruptcy and invited me to stop by to pick up my check for a penny on the dollar, which wouldn't have paid fuel expenses for the round-trip. There's a lesson in there somewhere for all of us.

Payment In Advance

To avoid situations where customers won't pay their bills, some crafters prefer to operate exclusively on a pay-in-advance basis. With this policy, the wholesale customer pays you before taking possession of the products. This saves a lot of hassle on all sides.

Payment in advance has an added benefit in that it creates a track record with your customer. It allows you to establish a history of financial honesty, after which you can decide on a case-by-case basis whether to extend the customer the courtesy of a net-30 credit. Some crafters require three payment-in-advance transactions before determining whether the customer can have the option of establishing a net-30 billing.

INVOICE

Arts & Crafts Unlimited

1492 Columbus Drive

Moon Valley, IN 54321

Phone: (123) 555-4545 • Fax: (123) 555-6767

Bill to:

_____

_____

_____

_____

Ship to:

_____

_____

_____

_____

Invoice #_____ Date_____

Customer Order #_____

Terms _____

Quantity	Item/Description	Price	Amount

Total Amount Due:

2% per month (24% APR) applied to the balance of all accounts after 30 days

INVOICE

Arts & Crafts Unlimited

1492 Columbus Drive

Moon Valley, IN 54321

Phone: (123) 555-4545 • Fax: (123) 555-6767

Bill to:

Woodwright's Gift Shop

P.O. Box 4231 Woodwright's

Cincinnati, OH 45210   1760

Ship to:

Bill Baily, Manager

Gift Shop

Old Stage Road

Cincinnati, OH 45212

Invoice #I-011507-4 Date May 23, 2011   Customer Order #

Terms _____ Net 30 days

Quantity	Item/Description	Price	Amount
10	Alder Mug Trees	$ 14.50	$145.00
5	Oak Cutlery Racks	12.20	61.00
2	Myrtlewood Clocks	65.00	130.00
10	Maple-Burl Plaques	12.25	122.50
1	Rosewood Tray	75.00	75.00
1	Laminated Jewelry Box	125.00	125.00
	TOTAL MERCHANDISE		$658.50
	SHIPPING AND HANDLING		65.85

Total Amount Due:	$724.35

2% per month (24% APR) applied to the balance of all accounts after 30 days

STATEMENT

Arts & Crafts Unlimited

1492 Columbus Drive

Moon Valley, IN 54321

Phone: (123) 555-4545 • Fax: (123) 555-6767

To:

Date _____

Terms _____

Account Number _____

Amount Past Due _____

Date	Invoice Number/Description	Charges	Credits	Balance
	BALANCE FORWARD ⟶			

Pay Last Amount
In This Column

2% per month (24% APR) applied to the balance of all accounts after 30 days

STATEMENT

Arts & Crafts Unlimited

1492 Columbus Drive

Moon Valley, IN 54321

Phone: (123) 555-4545 • Fax: (123) 555-6767

To:

Accounts Payable

Woodwright's Gift Shop

P.O. Box 4231

Cincinnati, OH 45210

Date _____ May 31, 2011 _____

Terms _____ Net 30 days _____

Account Number _00123_____

Amount Past Due _____

Date	Invoice Number/Description	Charges	Credits	Balance
	BALANCE FORWARD ⟶			$226.60
5-2-11	Invoice #I-01020-2	$291.50		$518.10
5-10-11	PAYMENT - Thank You!		$226.60	$291.50
5-16-11	Invoice #I-01150-4	$724.35		$1,015.85

Pay Last Amount
In This Column

2% per month (24% APR) applied to the balance of all accounts after 30 days

Purchasing

Purchasing is an ongoing process in any business. You will need to spend money on office supplies, craft supplies and materials, furniture and fixtures, office equipment, craft equipment, and tools.

It won't take long for you to get a feel for stocking office and craft supplies and materials and to know what items you need to keep on hand. You'll want to place orders regularly but will probably find monthly to be too frequent. I try to order quarterly because that keeps paperwork to a minimum and enables me to buy in money-saving quantities. Sometimes I buy more than a three-month supply to take advantage of sales.

Ask for Discounts

Unless you are already buying at rock-bottom prices, don't hesitate to ask your suppliers for better prices, especially local vendors, and particularly if you buy in quantity. For example, you shouldn't have to pay a local craft supplier the same prices that the casual walk-in does. You represent volume buying and repeat business. If the proprietor doesn't understand this, find another supplier.

Purchasing Wholesale

If you need a modest quantity of supplies to build your craft, it's fine to ask retailers for a discount, especially if you'll be buying on a consistent basis. But when your craft becomes a business, you'll need to obtain many of your raw materials in larger quantities. In this case, it becomes more cost-effective to skip the middleman and go directly to the source to buy your supplies, and purchase those supplies with a wholesale discount.

You may have to jump through several fairly easy hoops to set up wholesale accounts. To purchase wholesale supplies, you may also need a resale license (issued by the Secretary of State) in order to avoid paying sales tax. In return you'll need to collect and report sales tax either quarterly or monthly (again, this varies depending on your location). Your county business licensing division will be able to provide you with the necessary steps to get your license.

In addition, wholesalers may request references in order to establish a credit account. This is usually a single-page form that asks for businesses that can vouch for your reliability to pay your bills promptly. You can skip this step if you pay for all your supplies at the time of purchase.

While it may seem like a hassle to obtain a resale license and pay quarterly sales tax, it cuts your upfront costs significantly to buy your supplies wholesale.

Buying Office Supplies

When I started my business, I bought all my office supplies locally, but local vendors' prices eventually drove me out of town. Now I buy all office supplies by phone or online and save an astounding amount of money each year. Companies such as Quill (www.Quill.com) provide discounted office supplies. With the number of fine office supply companies available online, there is no reason to spend more than you have to with local vendors.

Buying Craft Supplies

Unless you live in a small town or rural area or use highly specialized craft tools and materials, you should be able to shop locally for many of your craft supplies. You need to shop wisely to keep your production costs down and your prices competitive. If local prices are too high and nearby dealers are unwilling to offer sufficient discounts, you have no choice but to go elsewhere for your craft supplies. And you will certainly have to shop out of town if you can't find what you need locally.

Some Internet research will yield a wealth of resources for craft supplies. Companies such as Michaels (www.Michaels.com) sell a wide variety of craft materials, and you may find many other specialized companies offering whatever supplies you need to keep your business running by googling "craft supplies" along with whatever specialized item you're looking for.

If you can afford the steep price ($250), an excellent resource for your bookshelf is *The Directory of Mail Order Catalogs*, published by Grey House Publishing (www .greyhouse.com/marketing.htm). This comprehensive resource is the premier source of information on the mail order catalog industry in the United States.

Is the Lowest Price Always the Best Price?

If you can get the lowest prices and great service, as I do with Quill Corporation, that's the best of both worlds, but it rarely works out that way. You often have to sacrifice one for the other. But when it's a close call, give your business to a local company.

For the first two years I was in business in Oregon, I gave a considerable amount of business to a local shop. I never got a nickel off anything I ever bought there, and when I asked the owner about a professional discount, all I got was a vacant stare.

A friend and local high school teacher recommended another shop he was dealing with. I no sooner introduced myself to the owner than he offered me a flat 20 percent discount on everything but sale items. Because his prices are generally higher than those at mail-order suppliers, I don't buy high-ticket items from him, but his prices on most materials and supplies end up being only slightly higher than my mail-order sources.

It's no more difficult to buy supplies by mail, and I would save a little by doing so. Nevertheless, I buy most of my supplies from my local dealer, and with good reason. When I need special services and I'm on a tight deadline, my local supplier is there for me as no distant mail-order supplier would be. He even opened his shop for me on a Sunday when I had an emergency and was faced with a Monday shipping deadline. Failure to meet that deadline could have cost me dearly in future business lost.

Sometimes the lowest price isn't the best price.

06

The Legal Aspects of Your Craft Business

Legal affairs, like filing, are necessary nuisances in every business. Although your craft business isn't likely to become entangled in all the legal debris many businesses must contend with, there are legal matters you must consider. The first is to determine how your business should be legally structured.

Sole Proprietorship

Most of us who work out of our homes are classified as sole proprietors. That is, we are the only principals involved in the ownership and management of our businesses, and we are the only ones responsible for the outcome. We *solely* reap the benefits, pay the bills, and suffer the consequences of liability.

Even if you now have or eventually will have other people working for or with you, you will probably remain the sole proprietor of your business. Having someone else working in your business in no way changes its status. As sole proprietor, you will be the owner and manager of your business, which has certain advantages and disadvantages.

Advantages of Sole Proprietorship

On the plus side is simplicity. There's not much to setting up a sole proprietorship. You aren't encumbered with endless paperwork, and you don't need a lawyer to advise you or create documents for the operation of your business. You pay taxes via your personal return—Schedule C of Form 1040—and your tax rates will usually be lower than corporate rates.

Disadvantages of Sole Proprietorship

Among the disadvantages of sole proprietorship is difficulty in obtaining outside financing, especially during the start-up stage. You will be entirely responsible for any legal and financial problems your business encounters. You will probably pay much more for health insurance than other, larger businesses do, and you will be able to deduct only that portion of your premiums allowed on Schedule A (Itemized Deductions) of Form 1040.

The vast majority of home-based entrepreneurs are sole proprietors. Be aware, however, that you're not bound to that status forever. But even if you eventually find partnership or incorporation advantageous, you will probably want to start out as a sole proprietor.

Partnership

When two or more persons go into business together, they usually form some sort of partnership. Partners share profits, expenses, responsibilities, and liabilities. They might own equal divisions of the business or have some other limited arrangement.

Partners enjoy the same tax breaks as sole proprietors. Each reports business profit and loss on Schedule C of Form 1040. It's fairly easy to set up a partnership and doesn't cost much in the way of attorney's fees.

Advantages of Partnership

Among the advantages of partnership for home-based businesses is the division of major equipment costs. For example, partners who work in the same crafts can share the costs of such major capital investments as stationary power tools, kilns, looms, and such, then work out agreeable schedules for the use of the equipment.

Sharing costs and the use of many high-ticket items makes sense because such equipment often stands idle much of the time. Partners can share computer hardware and software, expensive copying and duplicating equipment, and storage facilities.

The sharing of labor and brainpower can lead to lucrative and enjoyable ventures. Travel to and setup at craft fairs and other exhibits are much easier when there are partners to share the work.

Disadvantages of Partnership

Partnerships face the same financial difficulties and liabilities as sole proprietorships. Division of management responsibilities can lead to disagreements. And there are always potential problems when a partner leaves the business for whatever reason.

Persons considering partnership must breach numerous obstacles and work out many potential problems. Will the business operate out of one home or both? If one, which one? Will the partners carry equal workloads? How will they measure work? Will investments be equal?

Partnership Agreement

Any partnership requires a good written agreement. The better and more complete the agreement, the fewer the hassles down the line. Partners should spend time, individually and together, considering, discussing, and writing down everything pertaining to the business and partnership. Set everything you can think of in writing.

Give an attorney a copy of the document you and your partner or partners have created and set up a later meeting date. Your attorney should then draft an agreement for approval by all parties. After corrections, additions, and deletions, the attorney will draft the final agreement for the partners' signatures.

The agreement should make provisions for division of expenditures, profits, losses, responsibilities, and liabilities as well as prolonged illness, disability, or death of a partner. You must also consider the disposition of the share of a partner who retires from the business or leaves for any other reason. Include a buyout clause, and have your attorney advise you on restrictions pertaining to buying and selling of the business or any partner's share. You may want to include nondisclosure and noncompetition clauses.

The agreement can be revised or amended at any time and should be whenever the partners make major changes in the way the business is operated. Put it in writing, and keep it current.

Be sure to include language in your partnership agreement that details how a partnership can be dissolved. Having such language in place before partnering up can salvage a friendship, if not a business.

Limited-Liability Company

A limited-liability company is similar to a partnership but enjoys some of the advantages usually restricted to corporations. If you are thinking about forming a partnership, ask your attorney about the possibility and advantages of forming a limited-liability company.

Corporation

It's highly unlikely that you will want to consider incorporating when you start your business; in fact, you may never wish to incorporate. In the event your circumstances change, however, you should know something about the pros and cons. A good attorney and accountant will be able to advise you on this major step.

Incorporation can be expensive. You will certainly need an attorney's help, and you will have to pay your state a fee that might amount to $1,000 or more.

In a sole proprietorship or partnership, the principals are the business, and vice versa; everything that affects the business affects the owners. A corporation is an entity in and of itself.

Advantages of Incorporation

In a corporation, shareholders' assets are protected, and corporate assets are initially protected by current bankruptcy laws. Depending on the type of business, corporations generally find financing more readily available than sole proprietorships and partnerships do.

Disadvantages of Incorporation

On the downside, corporations are much more complicated and expensive to set up. Most pay high corporate tax rates. In general, a corporation faces more complications, with requirements for bylaws, a board of directors, corporate officers, annual meetings, and greater need for attorneys and accountants.

Zoning Ordinances

Municipalities and counties throughout the nation create urban and rural zones to allow, prohibit, promote, or discourage various activities. Certain areas and neighborhoods might be zoned agricultural, industrial, light industrial, heavy industrial, commercial, residential, or even such combinations as multi-residential or commercial-residential.

In some residential neighborhoods all business is prohibited, no matter what form it takes. Such restrictive zoning, however, is rare.

Obviously, you'll have no problem running your business in any industrial, commercial, or commercial-residential zone. Nor will county officials give you any trouble about operating in an agricultural zone.

Restrictive zoning of most residential neighborhoods is aimed at businesses that create noise, pollution, heavy traffic, and other activities best confined to industrial and commercial zones. Many allow professional and service businesses to operate, as well as any clean and quiet craft business, so you probably won't have any opposition to your running a home-based craft business. You need to be sure, though, so you'll have to check. Here, again, your local Small Business Development Center should be able to help. You can also check at your city hall or county offices.

Naming Your Business

Your business must have a name. It can be your name or part of your name with or without other elements, or it can be entirely made up, with no reference to your name.

If you have already decided on a business name—your own or an assumed or fictitious name—you need only determine what your legal requirements are (more on this follows) and how you should go about fulfilling them. If you're undecided, a helpful exercise is one writers and editors use when searching for just the right title. They list the possibilities and examine their merits. Let's take a look at how such a list might shape up for someone named Terry Johnson, who's trying to name a home-based craft business. Here are some possible combinations:

1. Terry Johnson
2. Terry Johnson Crafts
3. Terry Johnson, Master Crafter
4. Johnson's Crafts
5. Johnson's Craft Studio
6. Terry Johnson's Craft Shop
7. Terry Johnson's Crafts Unlimited
8. Terry Johnson's Craft Factory
9. Handicrafts by Johnson
10. Johnson's Craft Shop
11. Terry Johnson's Woodcraft [or other craft] Studio
12. Johnson and Company
13. Terry Johnson and Associates
14. Terry Johnson Arts-and-Crafts Enterprises
15. Crafty Creations

16. The Craft Factory
17. The Craft Company
18. The Arts & Crafts Factory

See how it works? By listing all the names that occur to you and simply switching elements about, within minutes you will have a working list. In an hour you could probably come up with fifty or more names. Just list as many as appeal to you; then begin eliminating those you like least.

The Internet is a wonderful resource for determining a potential conflict with your prospective business name—or a prospective domain name for a website. Type in your idea both with quotes ("Johnson's Crafts") and without quotes (Johnson's Crafts) to maximize the search efficiency and results.

Registering Your Business Name

Before picking a name for your business, you'll need to learn about any possible legal restrictions. Depending on state law or local ordinances, you may or may not have to register your business name; even if you're not required to do so, you may want to. Visit your local Small Business Development Center or chamber of commerce and ask for information about registering a business name.

Where I live, a person who uses what the rule writers call a *real and true name* as a business name need not register the name or pay a filing fee. A real and true name is defined as a person's surname with the given name or initials. My real and true name could be Kenn Oberrecht, Kenneth Oberrecht, G. Kenneth Oberrecht, or G. K. Oberrecht.

My state also permits the entrepreneur to add descriptive words to the real and true name without its becoming an assumed business name, which must be registered. If you add certain words that imply additional owners, however—such as *associates, company,* or *sons*—you may have to register it as an assumed name, as is the case in my state.

Let's take another look at the list of possible names for Terry Johnson's business and assume Terry has moved to Coos County, Oregon, and wants to set up a home-based business. Put a check mark by each of the listed names that won't require registration.

Numbers 15 through 18 are obviously assumed names and must be registered. Of the remaining names, numbers 4, 5, 9, 10, 12, and 13 would also require registration.

Even though number 14 would not require registration, it's a terrible business name. It's too long. Shortened to Terry Johnson Enterprises, it would still escape registration requirements but would then be too vague.

Once you've established a name for your business, the next logical step is to register it (or some variation) as a domain name for any future websites you set up. This is easy and inexpensive. I recommend using GoDaddy.com to register your domain name. I also recommend doing it as soon as possible so no one else snaps up your preferred domain name.

Mistakes to Avoid

In naming your business, avoid vogue words, slang, and clichés. Don't be too cute. There's nothing wrong with a good catchy name, but a fine line divides catchy business names from cutesy ones.

Stay away from names that are too obscure or esoteric for the general public or any that are otherwise inappropriate. The Bit & Blade might mean something to you but could be meaningless to most of your potential customers. Aardvark Aarts will probably get you listed first in the Yellow Pages but might also detour prospective customers who haven't the slightest notion of what kind of business you run.

You want your business name to be remembered. It should be easy to say and easy to spell. If you have a name like mine, I strongly recommend paying the filing fee and adopting an assumed business name.

Don't let your business name limit you. Johnson's Clock Shop meets all the essential criteria for a good business name, but what happens when Terry gets interested in marquetry or wants to expand into making toys, jewelry boxes, and wooden bowls? The name becomes obsolete.

Craft is a broad term that might not be quite specific or descriptive enough for some home-based businesses. Slight modification, however, can make it useful and direct. Johnson's Woodcraft tells the potential customer that here's a business that sells products made of wood, which can include anything Terry is interested in creating. Terry can also branch out into other areas of woodworking without fear of making the business name obsolete.

Licenses and Permits

Licensing requirements and ordinances vary among states, counties, and cities. Each state has different rules and regulations. The Secretary of State can tell you whether or not a business license is required for your state. Most states will require, at the very least, your business name to be registered with the state. You should also contact the Secretary of State for a resale license in order to purchase wholesale supplies without paying state sales tax.

You will also need to contact your local city hall for the specifics of running a business out of your home. As an example, a city may require a home occupation certificate which restricts the types of businesses permissible in residential zones. The rule of thumb for such restrictions is usually that the business must be "invisible to the neighbors at the property line"—this includes noise, commercial traffic, odors, and visible activity.

In Alaska I had to be licensed by the state. In Oregon there's no such state requirement. I live in a community consisting of the side-by-side cities of Coos Bay and North Bend. In Coos Bay I would have to have a business license; in North Bend I don't.

There's usually a small annual fee associated with business licenses or permits. Failing to be properly licensed, however, could cost you a stiff fine or even put you out of business.

Hiring a Lawyer

These days, lawyers are like ears: Most of us have one on each side. So it would seem that finding a lawyer would be as easy as turning left or right. But, like ears, not all lawyers are good ones.

Do You Need a Lawyer?

The important question is, do you need a lawyer? Let's hope you never will, but the odds are against that likelihood. Americans are the most litigious people in the world. No wonder—we represent only 5 percent of the world's population, but we have 75 percent of the world's lawyers.

Most start-up home craft businesses have no need of legal counsel, so don't panic and think you must rush out and put an attorney on retainer. If you find yourself puzzled over some legalistic aspect of start a home business, by all means consult whatever professional resources will help you along the way. But attorneys are expensive and often specialized, so make sure your need for legal counsel is serious enough to spend the money.

If you do feel the need to have an attorney on retainer, you must find a lawyer with a good reputation. Make an appointment, and discuss your plans. There should be no charge for this initial meeting, and you should feel no obligation toward the lawyer or law firm. If for any reason you're uncomfortable or uneasy with this lawyer, try another. In fact, you might want to meet with several before deciding which one would be ideal as your legal adviser.

Finding the Right Lawyer

The best way to locate prospective lawyers is to ask around. If you know other artisans and entrepreneurs in your community, ask who their lawyers are and if they're satisfied with the service they're getting. You can also check the Yellow Pages of the phone directory under "Attorneys—Referral," or phone your local Small Business Development Center. There's probably a toll free number available for the state bar association, which may have a referral service.

Many lawyers specialize, so you can narrow your choices by eliminating those prospects who work primarily in areas irrelevant to your needs, such as probate, divorce, juvenile, mortgage, immigration, bankruptcy, or personal-injury law. Look instead for a lawyer with a general practice and experience in contract and business law. The same lawyer will probably be able to handle your personal legal matters as well. Should the need for a specialist arise—say, for someone versed in patent law—your attorney will probably be able to refer you to a competent colleague.

Insuring Your Home-Based Business

An insurance agent should be more than someone who peddles policies and collects commissions, so you will have to shop around for the right agency and the right insurance companies. I use the plural *companies* because you will need several policies and might have to deal with more than one company. Independent agents, however, write policies for various companies, so it's possible to work with one agent for all your insurance needs. In any case, you should review your insurance requirements and policies annually and compare prices. Keep in mind, though, that every insurance agent is first and foremost a salesperson; your best interests are secondary.

Will Your Homeowner's Policy Suffice?

Homeowner's insurance covers your home. It is not meant to cover your business, even if your business is at home. If a customer comes to your house and slips on the sidewalk, it is very likely you will lose the court case because the insurance company can rightfully argue that you were not insured to run a business out of your home. So never have customers come to your place of residence unless you are insured specifically for that purpose with crafter's business liability insurance coverage.

For example, if you have customers in your home to pick up products, you might be able to get away with a studio coverage rider. This option is available on some homeowner's policies. Of course, you might not be able to get away with this. Such is the specific nature of insurance policies.

Your safest bet is to talk to your insurance representative and explain how you will be conducting business and what kind of insurance you will need to cover yourself. Remember, an insurance agent's job is to sell you insurance, so be aware that you may not need everything he suggests. Read the fine print on your policy to understand exactly what is and isn't covered.

Vehicle Insurance

Even though you already have insurance for your vehicle, this insurance will only apply to the *personal* use of your vehicle, not *business* usage.

Insurance agents would far prefer all businesses to have vehicles dedicated and insured exclusively for business use. In other words, they would like your van to be used solely to drive back and forth to craft shows, and never to the grocery store or to drop your kids off at school. However, most small crafters cannot afford a separately insured vehicle for business use.

The reality is, we all use our personal vehicle to conduct business, whether it's driving to a craft show or driving to purchase supplies. The important thing to remember is your insurance will *not* cover any business-related losses that might occur in case of an accident if your policy does not cover business use.

An insurance company cannot stop you from using your family car to drive to a craft show or go purchase supplies; but you therefore cannot expect the insurance company to reimburse you for lost sales, lost materials, or other business-related mishaps in the event of an accident. So if your vehicle is packed to the rafters with shelving units and products and you get into an accident on your way to a craft show, the insurance company is under no obligation to pay for damages to your stock or shelving units.

Because there is so much variability in insurance coverage and policies, it is best to talk with an insurance agent and describe what you feel will be the most accurate use of your vehicle. He or she can guide you to chose the policy that best fits your needs, and can assist you in learning what is covered by a policy and what is not.

Business Liability Insurance versus Business Insurance

If you decide to start looking into business insurance for your craft business, be very careful about the kind of policy you examine. *Business insurance* applies mostly to brick-and-mortar retail stores. Most crafters don't fall into this category.

Home crafters carry less of a risk than retail stores, so the policies should not be as expensive. You need to seek out insurance that covers *business liability*. This means if anyone is hurt in conjunction with some aspect of your craft business, then the insurance will cover the situation.

Remember, in-home businesses are a fairly new territory for insurance companies, and not all companies provide coverage. That's why you cannot trust that your homeowner's policy will take care of it if someone files a claim for a business-related incident occurring in your home. If your current insurance company doesn't cover an in-home business, you'll need to seek coverage from a company that does. Ask your insurance agent for quotes.

Disability and Health Insurance

If you're young and healthy, you should probably consider disability insurance. The older you get, and the more health problems you have, however, the higher the premiums will be. In fact, they quickly rise to prohibitive levels.

Similarly, the younger and healthier you are, the cheaper your health insurance will be. Regardless of your age or condition, though, as a self-employed person you can count on paying the highest premiums for the poorest coverage. Some professional associations offer group rates for their members, but don't expect any terrific bargains. From the standpoint of health insurance, your best prospect is to be married to a working spouse whose employer offers good family coverage.

Life Insurance

Life insurance is a complicated matter about which few generalizations are possible. You must assess your own situation to determine what kind of coverage, if any, you want or need. If your death and the loss of income from your craft business would create financial hardship for anyone, you probably need some kind of life insurance policy, either term or whole life. Talk to your agent about it.

Trademarks, Patents, and Copyrights

Most businesses are made up of physical property and intellectual property. Physical property includes business assets, such as office equipment, furniture, machinery, computer software, and vehicles. Intellectual property consists of company and product names and logos, inventions, and designs, as well as artwork, photographs, audiotapes, videotapes, films, and most written material.

We take many measures to protect our physical property. We see to routine maintenance and repairs. We lock doors and windows and may even install expensive security systems. We also insure our property against fire, theft, and other risks.

None of these precautions, however, adequately protects intellectual property. For that purpose we must use trademarks, patents, and copyrights—three distinctly different proprietary terms that share some characteristics.

Trademarks

A trademark is a name, logo, symbol, word, or graphic representation that a business uses to distinguish its products from those of other businesses. A company's services are similarly protected by a form of trademark known as a *service mark*.

The superscript symbols ™ and ℠ are used to identify trademarks and service marks that are not federally registered. The symbols serve notice to the public that common law protects whatever bears those symbols. When a business registers a trademark or service mark with the U.S. Patent and Trademark Office (PTO), it should then identify its product or service with the symbol ®, which designates federal registration.

You can register your trademark in your state or any state where you do business. It's a relatively easy and inexpensive process you can do yourself. Start by writing to the state attorney general's office and requesting the proper application form. Registration fees run from about $10 to $100 and probably average about $25. To protect a logo, product name, or service name, make sure you always include the proper trademark or service mark and note the date of its first use, which you will need to furnish when applying for other trademark registration.

If at any time you use or plan to use your trademark or service mark in interstate commerce, experts recommend you then file for registration with the PTO. In addition to the completed application form, you must submit a drawing of your trademark or service mark, three specimens of the mark as it is used in commerce, and the filing fee. A letter or phone call to the PTO will get you the proper forms and a copy of the booklet *Basic Facts about Trademarks*.

There's a good chance that state registration and common-law protection will suffice, in which case you won't have to register your trademark with the federal government. Even if you engage in interstate commerce, you may file for registration on your own, without hiring an attorney. I recommend, however, that you at least discuss the matter with your attorney, who should be able to determine how complex your trademark is and whether you will need further legal assistance. Even an attorney who's not a trademark expert can recommend one who is.

Trademarks last from five to ten years, after which they must be renewed to remain registered and protected.

Patents

A patent is an exclusive right a government grants to an inventor, a manufacturer, or an authorized representative to make, use, and sell an invention for a prescribed amount of time. In the United States a patent lasts for fourteen to seventeen years and is not renewable.

Persons engaged in the crafts business needn't be concerned with patents and patent law unless they have invented objects or created designs they think might be patentable. To pass the test of patentability, new inventions and designs must meet certain criteria, among them usefulness and utility. They also must fall into one of five statutory classes: (1) processes, (2) machines, (3) manufactures, (4) compositions of matter, or (5) new uses of any of the above.

Two of the three types of patents available in the United States are of potential interest to inventive artisans: utility patents and design patents. Utility patents, good for seventeen years, apply to new inventions. Design patents, which last for fourteen years, are for unique shapes or designs of existing types of objects.

If you have an invention to patent, you may prepare the application yourself, file it with the PTO, and represent yourself in the patent proceedings. But the process is extremely complex, time-consuming, and expensive. What's more, even if you are granted a patent based on an application process you completed unaided, it might eventually prove to be inadequate protection for your product or design.

My brother Phil is a founding partner in a busy Boise, Idaho, law firm. His practice includes a good bit of trademark work. He has worked to secure trademarks for his clients throughout the United States and in such far-flung places as Singapore and Sydney, Australia. When a client needs patent work done, however, Phil hires a patent attorney in New York.

If you want to patent something, I suggest you follow the good example of Phil and others and hire a patent attorney or patent agent. To practice before the PTO, a patent attorney must also hold a degree in engineering or physical science. A patent agent must have the same technical or scientific expertise and must pass the same examination patent attorneys take. A patent agent is not a lawyer, however, and therefore cannot represent a client in patent litigation.

Your attorney can probably recommend a patent attorney or agent or may elect to work with one in representing you. The PTO also maintains a directory of registered patent attorneys and agents. Check for a copy at your local public or college library.

Even if you plan to hire an attorney, I suggest you read the booklet *General Information Concerning Patents*, available from the U.S. Government Printing Office and possibly at a local library. Armed with the information contained in the booklet, you'll be able to ask your attorney intelligent and pertinent questions.

If you insist on trying to secure a patent on your own, then you will want to read *Patent It Yourself*, a hefty but readable book by patent attorney David Pressman.

Copyright

Copyright is a form of protection for original works that authors, poets, playwrights, composers, choreographers, artists, photographers, and other creators enjoy. It is afforded more or less automatically to any work, immediately on its creation in fixed form, and the copyright in the work normally becomes the property of the author or creator. In the United States, as of January 1, 1978, copyright lasts for the life of the artist or creator plus fifty years.

Filling out a form and paying the necessary fee to the U.S. Copyright Office does not copyright a work. Copyright is part and parcel of the creation process. If you create a work in fixed form, it is copyrighted and you own the copyright, unless you were an employee of a company and that company paid you to create the work, or you were not an employee but created the work under the terms of a work-for-hire agreement. Filing the paperwork and paying the fee *registers* the copyright.

There is no requirement to register a copyright, but it's best to do so as a way of claiming your copyright. Registration helps immensely if you ever need to sue someone for copyright infringement.

Copyright is available for unpublished and published works. It protects all unpublished works. It protects virtually all published works created by U.S. citizens and most foreign residents in the United States, as well as citizens of foreign nations that are signatories of one of the various copyright treaties to which the United States is also a party.

Among the various kinds of copyright-protected works, those you are most likely to create, use, or come in contact with in your business are literary works, photographs, graphic works, maps, audiotapes, videotapes, and computer software.

Some material is not eligible for copyright, including ideas, procedures, principles, names, titles, slogans, short phrases, lettering, familiar symbols, and typographic ornamentation. Most government-prepared material is also in the public domain and cannot be copyrighted.

Mere ownership of a work does not grant or imply copyright to the owner. Unless otherwise agreed upon in writing, copyright belongs to the *creator* of the work.

To illustrate, let's say there's a local artist whose work you particularly admire. As part of your business you buy lithographs of the artist's paintings, which you then mount, mat, frame, and sell at regional arts-and-crafts fairs. As the buyer, you legally own the prints. The people who buy the framed prints from you then legally own them. Both you and your customers are bona fide owners of the lithographs and may keep or dispose of them in any way, including selling them for a profit. But neither you nor anyone else may legally *copy* or *reproduce* the prints in any way without the artist's written consent. Regardless of the disposition of the lithographs, the artist retains the copyright.

Before 1978, to be copyrighted, most works had to be published with an acceptable copyright notice. Although virtually all works, published or not, are now protected, publication with the proper copyright notice is still important.

The Copyright Office defines publication as "the distribution of copies . . . of a work to the public by sale or other transfer of ownership, or by rental, lease, or lending." If you produce any kind of work that's eligible for copyright protection, it should bear the proper copyright notice.

As of March 1, 1989, use of the copyright notice became optional; before then it was mandatory. I recommend you follow the practice, however, because it offers certain distinct advantages. A copyright notice shows the year of first publication, which is an important reference. It identifies you as the owner of the copyright, and it serves notice to the public that the work is protected.

Moreover, if the copyright is infringed but the work carried the proper notice, the court will not allow a defendant to claim ignorance. Damages awarded might be as high as $10,000 per infringement, and in some cases could be up to $50,000. You may successfully sue for infringement even if the work did not bear copyright notice, but the claim can be deemed "innocent infringement" and result in greatly reduced damages—perhaps as little as $100.

A proper copyright notice has three important elements: (1) the copyright symbol ©, or the word *Copyright,* or the abbreviation *Copyr.*; (2) the year of first publication; and (3) the copyright owner's name. Example: Copyright 2007 Kenn Oberrecht.

Under the old Copyright Act of 1909, works could be copyrighted for twenty-eight years; then copyright could be renewed for another twenty-eight years, for a total of fifty-six years. For any copyrights in effect on January 1, 1978, the renewal term has been increased to forty-seven years, affording maximum copyright protection of seventy-five years. But such copyrights *must be renewed.*

Once a copyright expires, the work or property is in the public domain and may be freely used by anyone. Prior to January 1, 1978, improper copyright notice or failure to use a copyright notice on first publication often rendered works public domain.

Of the various ways to protect intellectual property, registering a copyright is the easiest. Filing the forms is not a complicated or tremendously costly process, and many of us do so without the assistance of an attorney. If I discovered someone infringing my copyrights, however, my first action would be a phone call to my attorney.

For additional information on copyright, visit your local public library. The Copyright Office will also send you a packet of publications on copyright, as well as the proper forms and instructions for registering copyright. (See the "Source Directory" at the back of this book, under "U.S. Government.")

Contracts

A contract is an enforceable agreement between or among two or more parties, permitting or prohibiting certain actions and activities, with mutual but not always equal benefits accruing to each party. Contracts of some form or another are used in most businesses.

Agent or Representative Agreements

If you plan to work with an agent or representative, you probably will be asked to sign an agreement stipulating that for each sale the agent makes, a share of the selling price (usually 10 or 15 percent) goes to the agent.

Traveling to the various trade shows is expensive, so agents representing artists and artisans often charge a nominal fee for each show. Details should be spelled out in the contract.

Agents also like to include exclusivity clauses in their contracts, which mean that you agree to sell your works only through that agent or that you agree to pay the agent's percentage even on works you sell without the agent's help. This is a one-way clause I don't like. My response to such a clause is, "Fine. I'll be happy to agree to the exclusivity clause, provided we amend it to say that you will devote your full-time efforts to selling my work exclusively and will not represent any other artist or artisan as long as you are representing me."

Of course, no agent will agree to such a preposterous clause, but it makes the point and sets a foundation for negotiation. Try to get any such clause deleted, severely restricted, or rewritten in such a way that it poses little or no difficulty for you. You don't want to get tied into a restrictive contract, for as long as a year, with an agent who turns out to be a lazy jerk.

Other Contracts

Some artists and artisans use work orders or job orders to set up contracts with their customers. These are simple forms that you fill in with all the pertinent information and customer's stipulations. They should be imprinted with your conditions and stipulations. When the customer signs the order and receives a copy of it, you and the customer then have a contract for a specific job.

You can have a local printer print work orders and other contract forms, make your own forms, or order them by mail. NEBS, Inc., has a number of such forms available and will imprint them with your name, address, and phone number. If you don't find one that fits your needs, NEBS will custom-print contract forms for you. Visit the website at www.nebs.com for more information.

Get Help

If you aren't accustomed to working with contracts, and you find their language baffling and full of unnecessary obfuscation, note all the confusing and confounding clauses. Then take the contract and your notes to your attorney for a translation. Pay close attention to what your attorney tells you, and soon you will learn to understand contracts without having to pay someone to interpret them for you.

07

Writing a Business Plan

A business plan is your blueprint for success. It's not something you devise and abandon once you're in business, but rather a working, changing, growing document and the basis for all your forecasting and goals.

A business plan is a detailed scheme describing how a proposed or existing business conducts its operations. In a home-based craft business, it's a strategy, worked out in advance, designed to define and delineate the ways the owner/manager will finance, operate, and profit from the business.

Your business plan also can be a document to use for attracting financial backing or selling your products and services to potential clients. Moreover, it can help you establish credit and credibility.

I had been operating my business full-time for five years when my wife and I decided to build the house we now occupy. My financial planning and forecasting helped me to prepare a convincing document that ultimately led to qualification for a home mortgage with a very attractive interest rate. It enabled me to expand my business from a small office and workshop to a comfortable and spacious work complex of about 1,200 square feet.

For most prospective entrepreneurs, a business plan may not be necessary unless you are seeking outside funding such as a loan or mortgage. As my example shows, a business plan can demonstrate to bankers or investors that you have logically and rationally examined the financial potential of your business.

Drafting a business plan requires careful thought, effort, and time. Don't try dashing it off over a weekend. Take the task seriously and give it the time it needs.

However don't let the task of writing a business plan dissuade you from starting your business. A business plan is a fluid endeavor that can grow and become more relevant as you learn how to run a business. Much of what goes into a business plan can be learned on the job, such as marketing. So it's your choice whether to write the business plan first, or start your business first. Again, this decision may depend on whether you wish to seek outside funding.

I must confess that when I started my business, I did not have a written business plan. I had a good idea of what I wanted to do and how I intended to accomplish it. Over the years I had also given a lot of thought to the business. I had studied, spent years in college, and researched the areas my college courses hadn't covered.

I'm not sure a written plan would have made a great difference in the early, part-time years of my business. Nevertheless, I'm convinced that a formal plan would have forced me to consider aspects of the business I ignored and would have alerted me to potential problems I could have averted.

The toughest part of writing a business plan is getting started. If you've read the first five chapters of this book and followed the directions there, you have already begun putting your plans and ideas on paper, and you should realize by now that it's not such a difficult process.

Writing a business plan is challenging and sometimes difficult, but it can be an enjoyable and enlightening exercise that hones your problem-solving skills and provides a foundation on which to build your business.

Why You Should Write a Business Plan

Of the various reasons for writing a business plan, not all apply to the home-based artisan. During the early stages of your operation—perhaps for the life of your business—you needn't worry about mergers, acquisitions, attracting highly skilled employees, or setting up strategic alliances with major corporations.

Your reasons for developing a good plan are more fundamental and pragmatic. Your plan should enable you to do the following:

- *Assess the feasibility of the venture.* You will eventually have to convince others that your home-based craft business is or will be a healthy, viable operation. The first person you must convince, though, is yourself. A good business plan is the most persuasive tool at your disposal for that purpose. In the final analysis, you'll be able to determine whether you should start your own business or keep your day job.
- *Evaluate your business resources.* Listing all your physical assets and professional attributes will enable you to determine what your needs are and

where your strengths and weaknesses lie. This can serve to reassure you and others and to steer you down the right road.

- *Evaluate your financial resources.* Before going into business, you must know what your financial status is and where you'll acquire needed operating capital. You should also have resources to fall back on in case of an emergency or in the event of an investment opportunity.

- *Identify potential customers.* You must know who your clients or customers will be to market your services and products to them most effectively. You need to identify your immediate buyers and target your future buyers.

- *Establish a workable timetable.* Once you have determined that your venture is feasible and evaluated your resources and markets, all that's left is to decide when to open your business. Also make some flexible decisions about growth and progress by plugging future plans into your timetable.

- *Set reasonable and competitive fees or prices.* How will you bill your clients or charge your customers? What do other local artists and artisans charge? You'll need to research fee and price structures thoroughly to ascertain what your services and products are worth and include that information in your business plan.

- *Provide a framework for scheduling.* Time study and scheduling are crucial to business success. You must know not only what any given project or product will cost you to produce, but also how much time it will take. Both short-range and long-range scheduling will continue as integral, ongoing processes for the life of your business.

- *Create a basis for forecasting.* Related to the scheduling process is a form of guessing known as forecasting. To forecast business trends, cash flow, and profit margins requires intelligence, experience, a thorough understanding of the competition, a firm grasp of markets, and a top-quality crystal ball. In the absence of the last-mentioned item, a good business plan is a reasonable substitute.

- *Facilitate the setting of realistic goals.* A business without goals is a trip without a destination—a time-consuming, money-wasting, aimless wandering. It's important to set goals from the start, and as you realize them, to set new ones. Your goals shouldn't be too easily attained or impossible to achieve. They must be on the tough side of realistic.

- *Land important and lucrative jobs.* If you have an opportunity to bid on a corporate or government job, the people letting the contract will want to know all about you and your business. You'll look like a bush-league player if you don't have a confidential business plan ready for limited distribution.
- *Secure bank or investor financing.* Although it's best to avoid borrowing money to run your business—especially during the formative years—you could experience a temporary cash-flow interruption or might need to buy some expensive equipment in order to land a job. A business plan can go a long way toward securing needed funds.

Organizing Your Business Plan

I can't offer you any rules or formulas for preparing a business plan. Just as no two businesses are entirely alike, no two plans can be identical. Business plans vary greatly, even within the same industry.

There's no set length or established format for a business plan. It can be as detailed or as abbreviated as you want to make it. Business plans for major companies might run to forty pages or more. I've heard of some reaching a hundred pages. Yours will certainly be shorter—probably somewhere between ten and twenty pages. But don't consider this absolute. Make it whatever length you're comfortable with.

As you begin listing information for your plan, include as many details as you can. Make the rough draft as long as it needs to be without padding. Then work it down to as precise and concise a document as possible.

Remember, a business plan is a working document about your operations; it should change as your business does. Consequently, it is not something that simply amounts to filling in the blanks on a form.

Business plan forms are indeed available from several sources. You'll find them in books on business and publications from the Small Business Administration, as well as in handouts from your local Small Business Development Center. There are even computer software programs available. All these sources—including the information in this chapter—are only guidelines, designed to help you write your own business plan.

Every business plan should be neatly typed or printed on top-quality paper, with 1-inch margins top, bottom, left, and right. Your business plan should have a cover page and a table of contents. It's also a good idea to include an executive summary. Other important sections should address such topics as organization, finances, management, and marketing. If you wish to include such ancillary documents as a résumé or brief autobiographical statement, credit references, and letters of recommendation, put them in an appendix at the end of the plan.

The plan should be divided into sections, with each section titled according to contents: Executive Summary, The Organizational Plan, The Financial Plan, and so on. Divide the sections with subheads.

Make sure everything about your business plan is as perfect and readable as you can make it. Misspelled words, misplaced punctuation, shabby sentence and paragraph structure, and errors in grammar and syntax leave a mighty poor impression. The implication is that if your business plan is sloppy, maybe your business practices are too.

If you're among the legions who have trouble handling the intricacies of American English, hire help. Find someone who can read your finished plan, locate the errors, and correct them. You'll need a consultant with above-average skills. Keep in mind, though, that just because someone teaches high school or college English or works as a writer or an editor doesn't necessarily mean that person is an expert in style, usage, and the intricacies of contemporary American English. In fact, finding such a person may well prove the most difficult part of creating your business plan.

Don't try to impress people with big or fancy words or with how much you happen to know about business or crafts. Avoid jargon, clichés, and buzzwords. Keep the language straightforward, simple, and clear.

Even if you are a skilled writer who doesn't need outside help, have someone read your plan and look for those elusive typographical errors and the little obscurities that make a sentence or paragraph cumbersome or awkward. Your plan should be pleasant and easy to read.

Cover Page

Center the phrase *Confidential Business Plan* at the top and bottom of the cover page, preferably in large boldface type. This is a message to anyone who reads or refers to your plan that the contents are not for general distribution.

About a third of the way down the page, center your business name, street address, P.O. box if you have one, phone number, fax number if you have a dedicated fax line, and e-mail address and website.

Then number each copy you distribute, for whatever reason. Keep a log in your business plan file that lists every person who receives a copy of your plan, the

Confidential Business Plan

Arts & Crafts Unlimited

1492 Columbus Drive

Moon Valley, IN 54321

Phone: (123) 555-4545

Fax: (123) 555-6767

E-mail: tjohnson@homenet.com

Web: www.artsandcrafts.com

Proprietor: Terry Johnson

Copy Number _____

number on that copy, and the date of distribution. This is another important message to anyone in possession of your business plan. It lets people know that you are keeping tight control of this document and implies that the recipient is responsible for safeguarding its contents.

Table of Contents

Provide a table of contents as a convenience to the reader. Simply list the various sections of your plan and their corresponding page numbers.

Executive Summary

Like the table of contents, the executive summary is provided as a convenience to your reader. Your business plan covers all aspects of your business in detail. The executive summary covers the same subjects, but in brief form. Try to distill the essence of your business into one page, with perhaps a paragraph devoted to each of the major sections of your business plan.

The executive summary is a courtesy to anyone who will be reading or referring to your business plan for whatever reason. In the minute or so it takes to read this one-page abstract, the reader can determine whether or not to read on or study the plan more closely. That makes it an extremely important part of the business plan.

Like the lead to a magazine article or news story, the executive summary must be as interesting, informative, and relevant as you can make it.

The Organizational Plan

In the organizational plan you'll lay out the specifics of your business organization. Start by identifying yourself and your business as a sole proprietorship, partnership, or corporation. Your home-based craft business will doubtless begin as a sole proprietorship, and chances are it will remain in that status.

If you have one or more persons working with or for you, be sure to include that information. Note whether these are full-time or part-time, permanent, or temporary employees or associates. Discuss their contributions to the operation of your business. If they're family members, mention that too.

You need to explain why your business exists and how it functions. Discuss its strengths, your business philosophies, and your craft skills. Resist any temptation to get technical.

Provide a clear picture of where you stand as you plan to launch your business and where you *intend* (don't use the word *hope*) to be a year from now, two years from now, and five years down the road. Demonstrate that you have immediate objectives and long-range goals. Write about the scope and direction of your business, and indicate what your scheduled operating hours and days are.

The Financial Plan

The financial plan is the most important part of your business plan. That's why two chapters in this book are devoted to financial planning and management. If you have read chapters 4 and 5 and prepared the financial documents covered there, you have already done most of the work required for this section of the business plan.

Statement of Financial Condition

Begin the section with a brief narrative statement of your financial situation, followed by a statement of financial condition, also known as a *personal financial statement* or *statement of net worth*. (See chapter 4, under "The Personal Financial Statement.")

For the beginning entrepreneur, this is the only part of the financial plan that can be precise. The rest of it is an educated guess at best, but you'll be called on to make such guesses more often than you might think, especially by lending institutions, the Internal Revenue Service, and probably your state revenue agency.

Sources of Funds

The Sources of Funds section is the place to divulge your financial sources.

The adage "It takes money to make money" applies to every business. You can't expect to attract clients or customers if you haven't carefully and wisely invested in assets and made plans to capitalize your business. What's more, investment and capitalization are continuing processes, lasting as long as you remain in business.

The chief function of a business plan is to provide an accurate appraisal of your business's financial health. This information will enable you to secure loans or entice financial backers; it should also make financial management easier for you.

Include a short report in your business plan called "Sources of Funds," which should list your assets, their worth, and their sources, as shown in the accompanying sample.

The Capital Assets Inventory form is handy for compiling the figures you'll need. Use a separate form for each type of property listed: furniture and fixtures, office equipment, shop equipment, studio equipment, and workshop or craft equipment. You need not include these forms in your business plan, because you'll summarize their contents under "Sources of Funds."

The completed inventory forms, stored with your insurance policies, are valuable documents should you ever experience a casualty loss, so it's important to update them regularly. If you must list or schedule certain property for insurance purposes or carry all-risk coverage for your equipment, be sure to send a copy of the appropriate form to your insurance agent each time you update it.

Sources of Funds

Assets	Amount/ Cost	Sources
Cash	$3,000	Business Savings
Investments	$15,000	Certificates of Deposit
Accounts Receivable	$2,000	Business Sales
Materials and Supplies	$1,500	Currently on Hand
Vehicle	$14,000/ $17,500	Installment Purchase
Furniture and Fixtures	$1,300	Currently Owned
Office Equipment	$5,200	Currently Owned
Studio Equipment	$400	Currently Owned
Workshop Equipment	$8,300	Currently Owned

Profit-and-Loss Projection

For the purposes of your business plan, prepare a profit-and-loss projection for the upcoming year on a monthly basis, then quarterly for the second year, and annually for the third, fourth, and fifth years. (For details, see chapter 4.)

If you are starting your business in midyear, project the remaining months of that year on a monthly basis. If you start your business in October, for example, you

Capital Assets Inventory Form

Type of Property _____   Date of Inventory _____

Description	Serial Number	Date Acquired	Cost or Value

TOTAL VALUE _____

Type of Property <u>Workshop Equipment</u>   Date of Inventory <u>May 31, 2011</u>

Description	Serial Number	Date Acquired	Cost or Value
Black & Decker Power Miter Saw	078539	1988	$185.00
Black & Decker Industrial Bench Grinder	001594	1989	125.00
Black & Decker Sander/Grinder	001138	1991	100.00
Elu Router and Router Table	EBD61493	1992	300.00
Toolcraft 41-4" Joiner/Planer	TCX5329	1994	275.00
Craftsman 10" Table Saw	SC88423	1994	400.00
Craftsman Belt and Disk Sander	SC00324	1995	275.00
Craftsman 13" Drill Press	SC01438	1996	225.00
Craftsman 10" Radial-Arm Saw	SC63115	2003	500.00
Craftsman Router Table		2008	360.00
Craftsman Industrial Router		2008	250.00
Craftsman Dovetail Fixture		2009	200.00
Alto'sPro Mat Cutter M.4590		2010	650.00
Assorted Power Tools			2,000.00
Assorted Hand Tools			2,500.00
Blades, Bits, and Accessories			1,500.00
Tool Cabinets			600.00

TOTAL VALUE _____ $10,445.00

should project profit and loss on a monthly basis for the first five quarters (or fifteen months), then quarterly and annually as described above.

Remember, a business plan is a living, working, evolving document. It should be a five-year plan that you review and modify as necessary—but at least once a year.

Balance Sheet

People accustomed to working with balance sheets will no doubt want to see one in your business plan. Prepare one according to the directions in chapter 4.

Cash-Flow Projection

A cash-flow projection will probably prove to be one of your more useful financial documents, so you should include one as part of your business plan. (Consult chapter 4 for details.) You might also want to discuss how you use profit-and-loss and cash-flow projections to manage the financial aspects of your business.

The Management Plan

In the Management Plan section, you must demonstrate your ability to manage your operation. Various business publications stress the importance of the team concept of management. They insist you list the various members of your management team and devote a half page each to a description of each member's strengths and management experience.

How Many Ponies in Your Show?

If you have other key people in your organization, by all means describe them. In your home-based craft business, however, you probably represent the entire management staff and labor force.

There's nothing wrong with the one-pony show, provided the star attraction isn't just a one-trick pony. So here's where you will need to tell about your show and all the tricks you know. You'll need to discuss your experience and diverse skills. Talk up your abilities and explain how your business will profit from them. I'm not suggesting you embellish the facts, merely that you uncover them and use them to your best advantage.

Discuss Your Skills and Experience

In the courses I've taught, I have worked with students who thought they had no valuable experience to build on, nothing worthwhile to offer. A brief one-on-one conference or interview, however, invariably turns up hidden talents and attributes.

To help you prepare a brief narrative statement, refer to your résumé, or make a list of the jobs you've held and duties you were responsible for. Be relevant. Zero in on jobs and duties that demonstrate management skills.

For instance, if, when you were a high school or college student, the state highway department hired you in the summer to pick up roadside litter, that's not relevant. On the other hand, if you were put in charge of a crew of summer workers picking up litter, that shows you have supervisory experience and indicates that you can handle responsibility.

If you have valuable craft experience, describe that too. Include amateur as well as professional work. Mention any awards, exhibits, or special recognition you've received.

You should even include any relevant volunteer or pro bono work and organizational offices you've held. All of this contributes to your business and personal identity and defines who and what you are.

List Your Business Associates

Even if you are the sole proprietor of a one-person operation, you have or should have professional or business associates you ought to list in your business plan. Provide the name, address, and phone number of your insurance agent, banker, accountant, lawyer, and any suppliers you work with.

Deal Intelligently with Your Weaknesses

Of course, you'll want to elaborate on your strengths as a manager and artisan, but you should also identify your weaknesses and describe the actions you'll take to eliminate them.

For example, if you plan to use a computer in your business and you've had plenty of computer experience, that's a strength worth discussing. If you have had no computer experience, perhaps you plan to take a course or two at a local computer center or community college or online. Or maybe you plan to learn on your own with books and instructional CDs or DVDs.

Weaknesses and insufficiencies are nothing to be ashamed of, but if you ignore them or fail to plan for their elimination, they remain an impediment to progress and success. Merely planning sensibly to shore up a weakness can neutralize its effect for the time being. Taking action as planned can turn a weakness into a strength.

The Marketing Plan

The first step in drafting a marketing plan is determining what, exactly, your business will provide its clientele in the way of products or services. You have probably already determined that. If not, you must do so now.

Identify Your Competition

Deciding what your craft business will sell will help establish your niche in the marketplace. Knowing this makes it easy to identify your competition and how you will deal with it.

Identify Your Markets

Developing a sound marketing plan requires market analysis. You need to conduct some methodical but fairly simple research to determine who your potential customers are and how many are out there.

If you intend to sell your products through local and regional galleries and gift shops, you need only determine how many such outlets there are in your area of operation to arrive at a base figure. You might also talk to the gallery and shop owners to get an idea of the number of customers they deal with monthly or annually.

If you intend to sell your craft items at arts-and-crafts fairs and other exhibits, show promoters should have figures available on how many people have attended previous shows and how the exhibitors have fared.

Perhaps you plan to sell your products through established mail-order sources. Any such company that accepts your products can provide figures on catalog distribution and order generation.

If an agent agrees to accept your work and represent you, ask for sales figures. Find out how many shops and galleries you can expect to do business with and how many trade shows the agent will attend. Gather as much pertinent information as possible and extrapolate the data as best you can.

The more numbers you can gather, the easier it will be to identify your potential markets and assess their worth.

Determine Your Market Share

Determining your market share is a bit more difficult, but, because it mainly requires guesswork, your figures can't easily be challenged. Be realistic and conservative in your estimates, and you'll probably outperform your best guess.

You will surely find that you don't have the capacity to take full advantage of your potential market share. For example, if you plan to sell through gift shops, galleries, and other retail stores and consider any such establishment within a day's drive to be in your range of operation, you might well discover 500 or more such outlets in your territory. How many of those do you think you could supply? Half? A fourth? A mere 10 percent would be fifty businesses and probably a more reasonable target. In fact, you may well find that to be more business than you can handle.

How many arts-and-crafts fairs are there annually within your territory? Find out, and while you're at it, determine which are the best. In the beginning you may have to hit them all as part of the learning process and in order to get your name and products known. Eventually, however, you will probably settle on several shows that consistently prove to be your best moneymakers.

Shortly after I moved to Oregon, I met and became friends with a high school art teacher who moonlighted at regional arts-and-crafts shows. He wanted to quit teaching and devote himself full-time to setting up and running a home-based business. When he decided to make the plunge, he continued selling his work mainly at regional shows.

For the first couple of years, he hit about a dozen shows a year, which is an exhausting, nearly impossible pace to maintain, but meanwhile he was able to make a living and build a mailing list of more than 10,000 customers. Ultimately, he settled on the three shows a year where, each autumn, he made about 75 percent of his annual income. He continued to work these shows while nearly doubling his mailing list. Now he's able to devote the first three quarters of the year to creating and developing products, running the lucrative direct-mail side of his business, and preparing for his show season.

His marketing plan was a good one. Not only has it enabled him to establish a smoothly running home-based business where he's his own boss, but in the meantime he has also gotten rich.

Your marketing plan should boil down to a fair assessment of the marketplace, how you will compete, who your potential customers are, what your market share amounts to, and how you will deal with growing demands on your business. After seeing to the necessary research and market analysis, put all this into narrative form and include it in your business plan.

Appendixes

You may or may not wish to include appendixes. If you have sterling credentials, though, you should seriously consider putting them into your business plan.

This is the place to include your résumé, a list of where you have exhibited and sold your works, a list of business and personal references, a list of credit references, and copies of letters of recommendation or commendation. If you have collected more than a few awards for your craftworks, make a list and include it here.

08

Taxes and Record Keeping

These days, it seems tax collectors are coming at us from every direction. Depending on where you live and do business, you may have to pay city, state, and federal income taxes; self-employment tax; personal property and real estate taxes; city, borough, county, or state sales taxes; state and federal fuel taxes; room taxes; and an assortment of other taxes disguised as user fees, license fees, application fees, registration fees, permit fees, and filing fees.

You will need to determine the kinds of taxes you must pay in your city, county, and state. If you don't already know, check with your local Small Business Development Center, chamber of commerce, or the local office of your state revenue department.

All of us must pay federal taxes, which we'll discuss momentarily. Because circumstances vary, even among people who are in the same business, and because tax codes and their numerous supporting documents exist in a constant state of change, it's impossible to provide specific advice. Furthermore, in the space of a chapter, I can provide only an introduction to taxes and taxation. I'll try to pass on some helpful tips and give you a grounding in the concepts so that you will be able to continue on your own.

In dealing with your taxes and essential record keeping, you can be involved at any level you wish, ranging from doing it all yourself to hiring others to do most of it for you. In any case, you need to understand what your responsibilities are. Even if you decide to turn everything over to someone else, you will still have to see to some tax chores.

Your options are several. You can do your own bookkeeping or hire a bookkeeper. You can prepare your own tax returns and associated forms and schedules, or you can have a professional tax preparer, accountant, certified public accountant, or attorney do it for you. The choices are yours, but I am going to make some recommendations.

First, keeping books is relatively easy, so I suggest you do it yourself, especially the first year or so you're in business. This will not only help you contain start-up costs, but it will also introduce you to the fundamentals of record keeping.

I continue to do my own bookkeeping after all these years because it helps me stay in touch with the financial aspects of my business and lets me know how I'm doing from month to month. What's more, a bookkeeper would be one more person I'd have to deal with in my busy life, and I'd rather not just now. Besides, by the time I've collected and sorted all my receipts, bills, canceled checks, and such, all that remains is entering the information on ledger pages and running the numbers through my calculator. With the right software you can even do it all by computer. It's no big deal.

I'm not about to tell you that doing your own taxes is easy. Far from it. It's a tedious, often confusing, sometimes infuriating task that just seems to get a little worse every year. Nevertheless, I recommend you try your hand at it as a way of learning about taxation and how it affects your business. I won't carry this recommendation too far, however. Once you've had the experience, decide for yourself whether to continue on your own or hire help. Learning how to keep books and prepare your tax returns will enable you to provide better, more complete information when you decide to turn it all over to someone else.

The tendency of most Americans is to put off tax chores as long as possible. Don't join the herd, especially if you decide to try preparing your own returns. You probably won't have all the documents you need until the end of January, so spend that month gathering all your essential forms, schedules, publications, and antacid tablets. Plan to work on your returns in February. That way, if you find you need help or discover that you don't have all the necessary documents, you'll have time and won't need to panic, or worse, pay a penalty for filing late.

Using Your Home as a Business

As a home-based crafts professional, you should be able to take a tax deduction for any rooms you use *exclusively* and *regularly* for conducting your business. These can include an office, a studio, a workshop, a storage room, a gallery, or combinations thereof. A studio, for example, need not be used exclusively as a studio but must be used exclusively as part of your business. My studio is a multipurpose room that houses my studio equipment, but it also has a desk and worktable where I do sorting and filing and see to much of my mounting, matting, and framing. Most of my reference books are on the bookshelves that line two walls of my studio. Along another wall are filing cabinets. So this room functions as a studio, library, and storage area, while serving other business purposes as well.

If you're planning to use only a portion of the space in a garage, basement, attic, or other large open area for business purposes, you might consider partitioning it to take advantage of allowable tax deductions. For example, you could partition off a room to use exclusively as an office or office-studio combination, thereby enabling you to take a business deduction for the square footage of that room, even though the remaining area may be used for personal or household purposes.

Another possibility would be to convert a spare room into a home office and partition off one corner of a basement or garage to set up a workshop. You could then take a deduction for the square footage of your office and workshop.

Similarly, you can take a deduction for a room you use for storage. You cannot simply put up shelves or cabinets for business storage in a room you use for other personal or household purposes, then take a deduction for that space. You can, however, partition off that space to create a separate room, thus making that square footage eligible for the deduction.

Use Test

You may be entitled to limited deductions for the business use of your home, but such use must meet certain criteria.

Exclusive Use

That portion of your home used for business must be used exclusively for such purposes in order to qualify for a tax deduction. You can't use a room as a studio, sewing room, and guest quarters, then claim a business deduction for it or any portion of it.

Regular Use

To meet the regular-use criterion, you must regularly use a specific part of your home for business, but "regular use" has more to do with continuity than frequency. For example, you might set up a well-sealed, dust-free, and adequately ventilated room as your paint room. Although you may work in your shop or studio every day, you might have products ready for painting only once a week or once a month. Provided that you use the paint room for no other nonbusiness purposes, it should be as eligible for a deduction as the shop or studio you use every day.

Principal Place of Business

Determining your principal place of business is a potential source of confusion. If you are a full-time home-based crafts professional, your home should qualify as your principal place of business, and the space you have set up for doing business should be eligible for a limited deduction. If you have a shop, studio, or gallery downtown, however, and decide to set up an office at home for seeing to various business tasks, your home office probably would not be eligible under the current regulations, because it is not your principal place of business.

Interestingly, though, the IRS recognizes the fact that you can have more than one principal place of business, provided that you're engaged in more than one business. For instance, if you teach carpentry full-time at a local community college and work weekends out of your home as a woodcarver, you could have two principal places of business: the college, where you are in the full-time teaching business; and your home, where you are in the part-time craft business. So you should be able to take the home-office deduction, so long as you meet the other criteria. Or you could be a lab technician, motorcycle mechanic, chef, plumber, cop, or computer programmer five days a week and run a part-time craft business from your home and still qualify for the deduction.

Separate Structures

The IRS also allows deductions for separate freestanding structures, such as a detached garage, barn, studio, shop, or storage building, provided that it's used exclusively and regularly for business. If you have any such structures on your property, they might suit your purposes. Keep in mind, too, that as your business matures, it might outgrow its space. Separate structures could prove the ideal solution to that problem.

Trade or Business Use

According to the IRS, "You must use your home in connection with a trade or business to take a deduction for its business use." Your home-based craft business should easily meet this criterion.

Calculating Your Business Percentage

The allowable deduction for operating a business from your home is based on the percentage of total home space your business occupies. It's a simple matter of arithmetic:

1. Determine the square footage of your entire home.
2. Determine the square footage of your business space.
3. Divide the square footage of your business space by the total square footage of your home; the result is your business percentage.

Example: Let's assume you live in a two-bedroom apartment of 750 square feet and convert a 10-by-15-foot bedroom into a home office and studio. Multiply the room dimensions to arrive at the square footage (10 feet x 15 feet = 150 square feet). Now divide the square footage of the converted bedroom by the total square footage (150 divided by 750 = .20). Your allowable deduction is 20 percent. If you live in a house of 3,000 square feet and use 1,000 square feet for business, your allowable deduction is 33.33 percent. You see how it works.

The IRS allows you to use any reasonable method to determine your business percentage. The one I've described is the most accurate and is certainly easy enough.

What You Can Deduct

Expenses associated solely with your living quarters and other areas of your property that have nothing to do with your business are *unrelated expenses* and as such are not deductible. These include repair and maintenance of living quarters and most appliances, landscaping expenses, lawn care, and such.

If you need to repair or replace a dishwasher or range, no portion of the associated costs is deductible. On the other hand, some seemingly unrelated expenses might be deductible. For example, if the furnace that heats your entire home breaks down, part of the repair or replacement bill should be deductible, according to your business-deduction percentage.

Costs associated solely with the benefit of your business are known as *direct expenses* and are fully deductible. If you put new carpeting in your office, paint your studio, or hang a new light fixture in any part of your work area, you may deduct the expense.

Most of the costs of running and maintaining your entire home are partly deductible as *indirect expenses*. They include mortgage interest, real estate taxes, utilities, trash collection fees, some telephone charges, insurance premiums, and the cost of installing and maintaining security systems.

Casualty losses, depending on their effects, can be unrelated, direct, or indirect expenses and are accordingly deductible or not. A grease fire that damages only your kitchen is a casualty loss but is unrelated to your business and is not an allowable business deduction. If a storm blows the windows out of your office, the casualty loss is directly related to your business and is fully deductible, less any insurance compensation. If a tornado delivers your roof to an adjacent county, the loss affects both your business and living quarters and is treated as an indirect expense, less any insurance or other reimbursement.

If you're a renter who meets all the criteria for the business use of your home, the business percentage of your rent is deductible. If you're a homeowner, however, no portion of your principal payments on your mortgage is deductible, but you should be able to recover these business costs over several years by taking an annual deduction for depreciation of the building and any permanent improvements to it.

Limitations and Reporting Requirements

Your allowable deduction, including depreciation, for the business use of your home is limited. In the simplest terms, deductions for the business use of your home are not allowed to exceed your net income. If they do, all or part of the deductions might be disallowed for that year, but those disallowed expenses may be carried over to a later year.

Form 8829, Expenses for Business Use of Your Home, is where you report all this information and where you will determine whether or not your expenses for any given year are deductible that year.

Business Use of a Vehicle

It's hard to imagine running any home-based business without using a vehicle. Depending on the nature of your work, you may need to drive only occasionally, or you could be on the road every day. You can buy a vehicle to use exclusively for business purposes, or you might enlist the family flivver for both business and personal use.

The IRS uses the term *car* to mean any passenger vehicle that does not exceed 6,000 pounds gross vehicle weight. That includes the kinds of vehicles most of us use for transportation: automobiles, vans, minivans, pickup trucks, and sport-utility vehicles.

Near Home and Away

Depending on the kind of craftwork you do and where you sell it, you might travel only locally or cover some distance to see to your business needs. Your business-home area includes the metropolitan, suburban, or rural area where you do business during the course of a normal workday. If you travel to and from a business location within the same day, that's considered local use of your vehicle, and costs associated with such use are deductible as *vehicle* expenses.

If business takes you away from home overnight or for a longer period, you must consider your vehicle expenses to be part of your *travel* expenses, which are recorded and handled separately and reported in a different section of Schedule C, Profit or Loss from Business.

According to the IRS, expenses for the local business use of your vehicle are deductible "if the expenses are ordinary and necessary. An ordinary expense is one that is common and accepted in your field of trade, business, or profession. A necessary expense is one that is helpful and appropriate for your business. An expense does not have to be indispensable to be considered necessary."

Vehicle Use Test and Expense Records

If you use a family vehicle for both business and personal purposes, business mileage must amount to more than 50 percent of the total mileage to qualify for the highest depreciation deductions. So you must keep good mileage records. How else could you know that of the 18,500 miles you drove last year, 12,580 were for business, allowing you to deduct 68 percent of your vehicle-operating costs?

You should keep a mileage log, but it needn't be anything elaborate. Note the date and odometer mileage when you place a vehicle in service. Also record the odometer reading on January 1 each year. Then for each trip, write down the date, destination or purpose, starting odometer mileage, ending mileage, and total mileage.

Your log can be a notebook or a ruled pad on a clipboard that you keep in your vehicle. You can also make your mileage log part of your business planner and calendar, either with loose-leaf pages or printed pages designed for such purposes. Printed vehicle logs are also available at office supply outlets.

You may elect either to take a standard deduction for each business mile you drive or to deduct actual vehicle expenses and depreciation. In the latter case, you should also keep receipts, work orders, canceled checks, and any other documents that substantiate your claims for expense deductions. You're not required to keep a separate diary or journal of vehicle expenses, but you may do so if you prefer that to recording expenses in a general expense ledger. In either case, you need not duplicate any information already contained on your receipts and other documents.

Mileage Log

Date	Destination/ Purpose	Starting Mileage	Ending Mileage	Total Miles

Total Miles This Page _____

Mileage versus Expenses

Whether to take the standard mileage deduction or deduct actual operating expenses is up to you. If your vehicle is inexpensive to operate, you might be smart to take the mileage deduction. You'll probably be better off deducting operating expenses and depreciation, however, if you drive an expensive gas hog.

In addition to keeping a mileage log, I recommend you record all your operating costs as well for the first year. At tax-filing time, do all the necessary calculations for both methods and pick the one that will give you the greater deduction.

Once you have determined the total miles and business miles driven for the year, divide the business miles by the total miles to arrive at your business percentage. For example, if you drove 10,935 business miles and 3,645 personal miles, total mileage for the year was 14,580. If you divide 10,935 by 14,580, you'll find that your business miles constituted 75 percent of the total. That means you can deduct 75 percent of your operating expenses and depreciation, or multiply the standard per-mile deduction by 10,935 and deduct that amount.

Leasing a Vehicle

Another option is to lease a vehicle instead of buying one. With a leased vehicle, you are normally allowed to deduct maintenance and repair bills, operating expenses, and lease payments. You may not use the standard mileage deduction, nor may you deduct for depreciation. You also need to log business and personal mileage.

Depending on the kind of lease agreement you sign, the IRS might require you to treat the leased vehicle as you would a purchased vehicle. If your lease contains an option-to-buy clause, the IRS may consider this a purchase agreement. So be careful with any lease and its wording. You may wish to seek assistance from the IRS or your attorney before signing a vehicle lease.

If the vehicle you lease has what the IRS considers an "excess fair-market value," you will also have to report an "inclusion amount" when you file your tax return. For information about all this, see IRS Publication 463, *Travel, Entertainment, Gift, and Car Expenses*, or one of the commercially available tax guides published each year.

Renting a Vehicle

Should your business require you to travel away from your business-home area by public conveyance, such as by plane or train, you might need to rent a vehicle once you reach your business destination. Your rental payments and operating costs are deductible as travel expenses, as are your plane or train tickets.

Other Deductible Expenses

Unless you take the standard mileage deduction, most expenses you incur while operating your vehicle for business purposes are deductible. In addition to fuel, repairs, and maintenance, they include but are not limited to bridge and highway tolls, ferry fees, parking fees, parking-valet gratuities, and towing charges, should your vehicle become disabled.

Fines for moving and parking violations are not deductible, nor are towing charges that stem from illegal parking.

Business Use of a Computer

If you buy a computer that you and other family members use for personal reasons, schoolwork, computer games, and other nonbusiness purposes and you also plan to use it for business, the IRS considers this *listed property*, and you will need to keep track of and distinguish between personal and business use. If your business use is less than 50 percent of the total use, your deductions will be limited.

Logging computer use is more difficult than logging vehicle use, especially if several people use the computer. For that reason and others, I recommend you purchase a computer, put it in your office or studio, and use it exclusively for business. In this case, it is not considered listed property, and you may treat it as any other depreciable business property.

All peripheral computer equipment and hardware and most software are also depreciable property. Compact discs (CDs), DVDs, printer, paper, printer cartridges, labels, and other essential computer materials are deductible as office supplies.

Business Expenses

Most of the costs of running your business are fully deductible in a straightforward way. As the sole proprietor of a home-based business, you will have to sort out the various deductions and report them on their respective forms: some on Form 8829, Expenses for Business Use of Your Home; some on Schedule C, Profit or Loss from Business; and some on Form 4562, Depreciation and Amortization.

We've already discussed deductions for the business use of your home and will more fully discuss depreciation later. For now, let's take a closer look at the kinds of expenses you will report on Schedule C. They include expenses incurred for advertising, business operation of a vehicle, interest paid, legal and professional services, materials and supplies, rent, leases, repairs and maintenance, taxes, licenses, permits, travel, some meals and entertainment, dues to professional associations, some publications, printing and photocopying, postal costs, freight, express and parcel services, trash collection, and others you'll no doubt discover.

Keeping Receipts

Keeping receipts is not the odious chore so many people think it is. It's mainly a matter of developing the habit of collecting receipts for all your business purchases. For most of your expenses, receipts are automatic by-products of your various transactions. Your telephone, utilities, and other monthly bills are receipts you'll need to keep. When you gas up your vehicle, keep the credit card receipt; if you pay cash, ask for a cash receipt. When you're on the road, get receipts for all your food, lodging, and other expenses.

If you buy office and craft supplies in quantity, you'll keep the number of receipts to a minimum. Set up accounts with vendors and you'll also save time and trouble by paying and filing monthly statements.

Even when you get all this under control, you will still occasionally need to buy some supplies at supermarkets, drugstores, and discount outlets. Just make sure you get a cash register receipt. Many register receipts itemize purchases, and all provide dates and amounts. When you get a register receipt that doesn't display all the essential information, fill it in yourself, immediately.

I make a habit of marking receipts as I get them and noting any important information. I use a red pen to circle the date and amount paid. If the receipt isn't itemized, I write down what it was for: hardware, varnish, glue, paper clips, lunch, and so on. This helps me zero in on the information I need when I do my bookkeeping.

When I pay my stacks of monthly bills, I note the date and circle the amount paid, but I don't bother writing the check number on the bill, because that will be in my check register if I need it. While I'm at it, I put a red X in the check register at each check I write that goes to pay for an expense for which I don't have an adequate receipt. The canceled check is then my receipt.

No matter how careful you are, you will sometimes forget to ask for a receipt, or you might lose one. In that case, make your own receipt at once, noting all the pertinent information. This should be acceptable to the IRS. What's important is that you write the receipt while everything is fresh in your mind, not at the end of the month when you do your bookkeeping.

Depreciation of Business Property

The purchase of certain equipment, tools, furnishings, and other property you use in your business is considered a capital expenditure, not normally eligible for deduction as an expense for a given tax year. Rather, it must be treated as depreciable property, with the cost deducted gradually over a number of years. Normally, this includes any property that has a useful life of more than one year.

In addition to vehicles and computers, already discussed, other depreciable property you will probably use in your home-based craft business includes the following:

- *Furniture and fixtures* for your office, studio, and workroom.
- *Office equipment*, such as a computer, calculator, copier, fax machine, and telephone.
- *Craft equipment*, including power tools, sewing machines, kilns, and such.
- *Buildings* not used for residential purposes, including the business portion of your home.

Property Classes and Recovery Periods

Depreciable property is classified according to the number of years you must normally take to depreciate it or write it off. Because of the conventions you're required to use in calculating depreciation, recovery periods run a year longer than their respective classifications. For example, so-called five-year property will remain on your books for six years, seven-year property for eight.

Any machinery you use—including office and workshop equipment, computer equipment, and vehicles—is five-year property. Desks, chairs, filing cabinets, bookcases, tables, and other furniture and fixtures you use in your business are seven-year property.

Congress keeps extending the recovery period for nonresidential real property. In 1993 it was increased from 31.5 years to 39 years. By the time you read this, it could be even longer. The annual deductible rate for 39-year real property is 2.5641 percent, except for prorated first and last years.

Section 179 Deductions

Section 179 deductions are an exception to what we've been discussing. Certain tangible personal property used in business is eligible to be treated as an expense and may be fully or partly deductible for the tax year. At this writing, you may deduct up to $105,000 of the cost of such property as office equipment, craft equipment and machinery, computers, and computer peripherals. This amount changes frequently.

Your business vehicle is eligible, provided it was not previously used as a personal vehicle and then converted to business use. The Section 179 deduction for qualifying vehicles is also limited.

Buildings are not eligible for Section 179 deductions.

You can use this information to your advantage by paying close attention to your earnings and expenses. If you have a better year than you anticipated, you might need all the immediate deductions you can legally take to reduce your taxable income. This is a good time to look for possible 179 deductions. If your income turns out to be lower than you expect and you have plenty of deductions, you probably won't want to take the Section 179 deductions, even if you have purchased eligible property. Normal depreciation procedures will extend your deductions into future years, when, presumably, your income will be higher.

Reporting Depreciation

Enter all pertinent depreciation information on Form 4562, Depreciation and Amortization. Once you have calculated your allowable depreciation, enter the total on Schedule C.

Surmounting all the obstacles and wading through the mire of instructions for figuring depreciation can make for a difficult trip. This single aspect of taxation may be troublesome enough to make you seek the services of a tax professional.

If you want to try it on your own, you should consult IRS Publication 334, *Tax Guide for Small Business*. Some of the commercially available guides, such *as J. K. Lasser's Your Income Tax*, are much more readable and relatively free of bureaucratic gobbledygook.

Estimating Your Taxes

Uncle Sam does not like to have money owed to him at the end of the year, so we're required to keep our taxes paid up. Under a simpler, saner system, it would be easy to do the bookkeeping at the end of the month, deduct a reasonable percentage from profits, and mail the old guy a check. But Uncle also dislikes simple and sane systems. So we have yet another form to fill out and file quarterly and another exercise in exasperation.

If you're working part-time at this business and full-time elsewhere, you can increase the amount your employer withholds from your paycheck to keep from owing taxes at year-end. You could have a working spouse do the same, if you file jointly. Otherwise, you will have to estimate your income and taxes, file Form 1040-ES, and pay your estimated taxes quarterly.

Filing the forms is the easy part; figuring out what to put on the forms is the hard part. When you first encounter this obstacle, you'll ask the same question the rest of us did: How can I possibly know what I'm going to earn in the future? Then you'll do what the rest of us did: Guess.

If you've worked at your business part-time, you can use your records to extrapolate income and expenses and at least come up with a figure.

Safe Harbor

IRS regulations provide what is known as a "safe harbor" for estimating taxes and avoiding penalties. As of 1994 self-employed individuals with prior-year adjusted gross incomes of $150,000 or less are permitted to base their estimated-tax payments on 100 percent of their prior-year tax liability. Those with adjusted gross incomes exceeding $150,000 may base their estimations and payments on 110 percent of their prior-year tax liability.

You are not required to use the safe harbor, but if you elect not to, your estimated-tax payments for the current year will have to equal at least 90 percent of your prior-year tax liability. Otherwise, you could be charged a penalty.

Record Keeping

As a self-employed taxpayer, you may use either the accrual or the cash accounting basis. With the accrual basis, you report income as it is earned, not as it's received. You also report expenses on the dates you incur them, not necessarily on the day you pay them. With the cash basis, you report income when you are paid and costs as you pay them.

Advantages of Cash Basis

Cash accounting is definitely the simpler method. It also offers certain advantages that can save you tax dollars. For example, at the end of a high-income year, you may elect to delay your billing until late December or early January in order to defer payment of money owed you into the coming tax year, thus reducing your taxable income for the current year.

No Set Rules for Records

You must keep accurate records of all your income and all your expenditures. There are no set IRS requirements, however, for how you set up your books, as long as you maintain written records or computer records you can print out.

If you do your own taxes, you might want to visit an office supply outlet to examine available commercial accounting and record-keeping systems, or you could devise something yourself. If you own a computer, you may wish to review some of the many software programs available for business and personal financial management and record keeping.

A Simpler Bookkeeping System

I use a simple manual bookkeeping system I devised when I first went into business part-time. It has served me well for years, keeps me informed, and is housed in a single three-ring loose-leaf binder, which is organized with index tab pages. The ledger pages are created from my handy-dandy four-column pads.

To keep track of income, I label the top of a page *Income*, followed by the year. The narrow left column is labeled *Date*, the wide column *Source*, and the four accounting columns, respectively, *Amount*, *Month*, *Total for Month*, and *Cumulative Total*.

As checks arrive I enter the date, source, and amount. At month's end I write the month in the second column, income for the month in the third column, and a running cumulative total in the fourth column. I record all reimbursed expenses the same way on a page that's identical except for the title.

For recording most of my expenses, my ledger has index tabs and pages labeled *Vehicle, Office, Repairs & Maintenance, Dues & Publications, Photo Supplies, Shop Supplies, Printing & Photocopying, Postal, Freight & Shipping,* and *Miscellaneous*. For each of these categories, I prepare the page with *Date* in the far left column and *Item* in the wide column. I then label the four accounting columns *Cost, Month, Total for Month,* and *Cumulative Total*.

Income/Expenses Worksheet

Date	Source (or Item)	Amount or Cost	Month	Total for Month	Cumulative Total

Several categories call for special handling. For example, my *Travel & Entertainment* pages reflect certain IRS requirements as well as my own need to see how I spend my money. I label the four accounting columns *Meals & Entertainment, Transportation, Lodging,* and *Miscellaneous.* After each trip I subtotal each column. The IRS allows a deduction for only a percentage of meals and entertainment, which the ledger page keeps separate.

On another page titled *Utilities, Phone, & Trash,* I label the wide column *Month,* under which I list the twelve months. The four columns are for *Electric, Water, Phone,* and *Trash.* Totals for electric, water, and trash get adjusted by my business percentage. I adjust my phone charges as I review my monthly bills.

If you have only one phone line coming into your home, the IRS does not allow a deduction for that line but does allow the deduction of long-distance business calls. If you put a second phone line or a dedicated fax line into your office, you may deduct charges for that.

I have four insurance policies that are directly or indirectly related to my business. The insurance page in my ledger has columns for *Vehicle, Boat, Homeowner,* and *Mortgage.* I report costs for my vehicle and boat insurance on Schedule C, adjusted homeowner's and mortgage insurance on Form 8829.

For depreciation, I make ledger pages for various kinds of property. Although I could keep all five-year property together and all seven-year property together, I prefer to categorize further. For example, I have pages labeled *Books & Software (5-Year Property), Machinery & Equipment (5-Year Property),* and *Furniture & Fixtures (7-Year Property).* I also keep the records for my business vehicle on a separate page, labeled *Vehicle (5-Year Property).*

The far left column of each depreciation page is labeled *Date,* the wide column *Item,* and the first accounting column *Cost.* I leave the other columns untitled until year-end. If I elect to expense any of these items as a Section 179 deduction, I so note it on the page for future reference. If I depreciate property, I then use the other columns, showing the current year and percentage allowed at the head of column two. The following year I enter the year and percentage at the head of column three, and the year after I use column four. Sometimes there's sufficient room to continue adding the out-years at the bottom of the same page. When there's not, I just add another page.

I try to keep up with all this by doing my bookkeeping monthly, but sometimes I'm too busy and must put off the job for a month or so. At the end of the year, I run my column totals and do all the necessary calculating to make my books ready for filling out my tax forms.

Capitalizing Start-Up Costs

To qualify for a deduction of the preliminary costs of starting a business, the IRS requires those costs to be capitalized over time. Some of these costs might not be deductible until the business terminates. All of this can lead to some complicated and time-consuming record keeping.

For big companies making major investments in equipment and materials, the record keeping and procedures are necessary for taking the concomitantly large deductions. For the home-based entrepreneur, however, the puny deductions are hardly worth the hassles.

You can simply elect not to take any deductions for start-up costs. You won't have to do all that bookkeeping, and you won't run afoul of IRS regulations. Just make sure you keep your start-up costs low. Anything you buy before you are in business is the kind of expenditure that would have to be capitalized to be eligible for deduction. Once you've made a sale, however, you are officially in business and may then begin deducting expenses in the same tax year they occur.

Of course, you will want to use tools and materials you already have on hand; you just can't take deductions for them if you want to avoid the capitalization hassles.

My recommendation is to keep your start-up costs minimal and make a sale as soon as possible. Don't buy new office furniture and equipment or lay in large quantities of materials and supplies before you've sold anything. Operate on a shoestring until you make a sale; then begin purchasing the necessities for your business, keeping all the receipts and maintaining careful records of all expenditures.

Sales Tax

Depending on the nature of your business and your state's requirements, you may have to apply for a license to collect sales tax on the items you sell.

If your state has a sales tax, you could be required to collect taxes on items you sell directly to customers at arts-and-crafts shows, craft fairs, and similar events. On the other hand, you probably won't have to collect taxes on items you sell through shops, galleries, stores, or any other retail outlets where the proprietors of those businesses collect taxes from their customers. Similarly, you should be exempt from paying sales taxes on raw materials and finished products that you purchase for

Useful Publications from the IRS

Number	Title
17	Your Federal Income Tax
334	Tax Guide for Small Businesses
463	Travel, Entertainment, Gift, and Car Expenses
505	Tax Withholding and Estimated Tax
521	Moving Expenses
523	Selling Your Home
525	Taxable and Nontaxable Income
526	Charitable Contributions
533	Self-Employment Tax
535	Business Expenses
536	Net Operating Losses
538	Accounting Periods and Methods
541	Partnerships
542	Tax Information on Corporations
544	Sales and Other Dispositions of Assets
550	Investment Income and Expenses
551	Basis of Assets
553	Highlights of (the Year's) Tax Changes
560	Retirement Plans for Small Business
561	Determining the Value of Donated Property
583	Starting a Business and Keeping Records
587	Business Use of Your Home
590	Individual Retirement Arrangements (IRAs)
946	How to Depreciate Property

resale. The idea here is to prevent what would amount to multiple taxation on the product as it progresses through the stages of manufacture.

You'll need to determine your state's requirements, so check with your local chamber of commerce or Small Business Development Center. You can also get information from your state's revenue department.

Hiring a Tax Professional

So in the final analysis, once you know the ropes and are documenting your expenses and income on a regular basis, should you do your own taxes or should you hire a tax professional?

For the small craft business, the latter is the easiest course. Taxes are an unbelievably complicated and sophisticated field of expertise. Starting a home business is difficult enough without expecting the added load of becoming a tax expert and staying up to date on regulations as well.

That said, you *should not* just plan to visit the walk-in tax services that spring up in every mall come March. Tax professionals often specialize in various disciplines, and you will need the expertise of someone who works with home businesses. These professionals are skilled in letting you know what's deductible and what's not, and may offer valuable advice on how to maximize your business practices from a tax perspective.

Tax experts can save you a great deal of money over the years, and benefit they provide can far surpass any annual fee for filing your taxes.

IRS Forms You'll Probably Need

Form	Title
Form 1040	U.S. Individual Income Tax Return
Form 1040-ES	Estimated Tax for Individuals
Form 4562	Depreciation and Amortization
Form 8829	Expenses for Business Use of Your Home
Schedule A	Itemized Deductions
Schedule B	Interest and Dividend Income
Schedule C	Profit or Loss from Business
Schedule D	Capital Gains and Losses
Schedule SE	Self-Employment Tax

09

Using a Computer in Your Business

Your computer and Internet connection unquestionably will be one of the most powerful tools in the development and marketing of your craft business. In addition to using such software applications for record keeping and inventory, there are endless options for taking advantage of marketing and advertising opportunities online.

It's a brave new world of Internet possibilities out there. If there's one thing upon which both computer-literate and computer-illiterate crafters can agree, it's that there are far more powerful marketing tools available online than there were even five years ago. Most of these tools do not require a bachelor's degree in computer science to operate. Almost without exception, even the technophobes among us can learn to use them within an hour or two.

And most of them are free! In this economy, it would be foolish to waste the amazing networking and marketing potential of the Internet, which can help you earn money from your craft. Your exposure can be international rather than limited to your small corner of the world. Having an Internet presence is like having five or six full-time salespeople who never sleep.

Websites

If you're a crafter, chances are you'll want a website. Websites have a number of huge advantages over a traditional brick-and-mortar storefront.

One obvious advantage is cost. The most expensive website is usually far cheaper than the cheapest storefront. Rather than paying property taxes or rent and spending endless time fiddling with window displays and store layout, you can spend as little as minutes a week (perhaps less) to update your website.

Another huge advantage of a website is that it negates geographical barriers. The success of a storefront is limited by how many people walk through the door. But if your store is located in the middle of Iowa and a potential customer is located in New Zealand, you're not likely to cross paths.

A website eliminates that distance. Customers from all over the world can log on to your site and see your products.

There are two basic types of sites for a crafter: informational and sales. Informational websites are just that: places where potential customers can go to learn more about your craft, find out how you make it, read a little about your personal life, see photos of the production process, or learn anything else you feel would be of interest to them. You can post what craft shows you'll be attending and/or contact information for buying your product.

Sales websites are more complicated because you need to be able to set up payments from customers. Depending on how you do this, you will be required by law to provide security features so hackers can't steal credit card numbers or other personal data. The simplest way to do this is to utilize the built-in security features of PayPal or other services which process financial transactions.

Webmaster or Not?

Do you need a webmaster to create your website? The answer depends on a number of factors.

How familiar and comfortable are you with computers? Many older crafters who didn't grow up in the age of computers may still be uncomfortable navigating the electronic terrain. In this case, there are endless numbers of computer geeks who would be happy to do it for you. Ask around and get recommendations. Naturally you'll want to work closely with your webmaster to make sure the site is exactly how you wish it to be.

But even for those unfamiliar with the mysteries of computer coding, setting up a site can be surprisingly easy, especially if you utilize a free website service (type "free website builder" into your Internet search engine). These services, such as Weebly.com or Moonfruit.com, provide premade templates and customizing features such as drag-and-drop components. You can add text, photos, embedded videos, new pages, etc. The results can be surprisingly professional.

Domain Names

One of the first things you may wish to do before establishing an online presence is to register a domain name. A domain name is a specific web page locator (address) that belongs to you and you alone. For example, the domain name www.google. com belongs to the Google search engine company. Such services as GoDaddy.com or Register.com are easy to use for registering your domain name. They are also inexpensive, as long as you resist purchasing all the extra bells and whistles companies urge you to consider.

The difficulty might lay in finding a domain name that's available. Fortunately, the registration services can search this out within seconds.

Have a list of potentially acceptable domain names ready when you register. Remember, the domain name does not necessarily have to correlate exactly with your business name. For example, if your business is called "Terry Johnson Crafts," then www.terryjohnsoncrafts.com may not be available. In this case, consider registering www.craftsbyterryjohnson.com or some other variation. Even a more esoteric connection such as www.mycraftworkshop.com can work, as long as the search engines pick up the key words that will associate the website with your particular craft.

In designing a website, it's tempting to use every possible clever visual trick to catch a browser's eye—sparkles and animated gifs and fussy wallpaper and other gizmos. However, as marketing experts will tell you the more cluttered and busy something is, the less a browser will focus on. So keep your website clean and uncluttered so that potential buyers will truly see what you have to offer.

Additionally, many people still use older browsers on their computers. The more complex your site is in terms of sparkle and pizzazz, the greater the possibility that some customers will not be able to fully load or utilize your site.

E-mail

Probably the single most important feature you can set up once you have an online presence is an e-mail address. Most business web pages hosted by Internet service providers (ISPs) will have e-mail addresses available that will be tied to your domain name (such as terry@terryjohnsoncrafts.com) as a standard part of the hosting fee. You can also set up an anonymous e-mail address through Google or Yahoo.

Regardless of how you approach it, getting an e-mail address dedicated to business use will make it that much easier for customers to reach you. It has the added bonus of being more secure, since it's not always a good idea to post a phone number online for anyone to see.

Search Engines

A search engine directs potential customers to your website through the use of certain key words. How many times have you typed "wooden trains" or some similar phrase into Google to see what sites come up? Now you are operating from the other side of that equation: You want your site to come up in response to certain key words as well.

Search engines do just what the name implies. They search web pages, blogs, and other informational Internet locations for content. When you tell Google (or any other search engine) to find web pages that contain information about wooden trains, Google will provide a list of these sites, based on both the terms requested as well as the popularity of the site (determined by the number of previous requests). While each search engine uses different formulas to determine which page gets the highest ranking, it is usually a combination of these two data sets: relevance to requests and popularity.

Blogs

Another powerful and free tool is a blog. Blogs and websites can work in tandem, but a blog is much easier to modify than a website, so it can be updated frequently and with very little effort. Blogs are easy to create and are free through such hosting sites as blogspot.com or wordpress.com.

Blogs have become the cyber equivalent of the back fence, but with no geographical limitations. You can post chitchat about how a craft show went (with photos to accompany the text), items of personal interest, compliments you've received, a new product you're ready to launch, or other items related to your business. Keep the tone upbeat and cheerful—this is not the place to post criticism of another crafter or frustration over bad sales at a show. A blog dedicated to your business is also *not* the place to post personal information unassociated with your business, such as photos of your vacation or the birth of your new grandson, cute as he may be.

But a blog *can* be a place to be less formal and more casual, a place where customers can see your "human" side—and it's the human side of a business that can forge connections with potential customers. You might post some work-in-progress images, for example. The important thing is to personalize the blog with your experience. Try to stay away from hard selling, since this is easily identifiable and will turn some people away.

Nothing says you can't check out other blogs and comment on them in a way that includes a link to your blog or website. Most people don't mind your including a web address as long as the comment is positive and relevant. Avoid being mean-spirited, since that can negatively impact your own blog.

If you're confident in your speaking ability, BlogTalkRadio.com is a growing Internet radio social network that can allow you to reach listeners around the world.

Learn to utilize the full benefits of your blog by incorporating video or audio clips, as well as links to other relevant posts. Without going overboard, photos or other illustrations are helpful to break the visual monotony of lots of text.

YouTube

Once you have an online presence, you can market yourself further by taking advantage of other media. Many crafters have made videos of some aspect of their business, and then posted those videos on YouTube. You can also embed YouTube videos on your own site. Videos might demonstrate how a customer can use your craft, some of the sophisticated construction techniques you use in making your craft, or other items of interest to customers. In this computer age, photos and video clips and other visual aids can boost interest in your product tremendously.

Social Networking Sites

The explosive growth of Facebook, MySpace, and other social networking sites has been of immeasurable help to crafters by allowing them to connect with friends, customers, and professional associations with the greatest of ease.

Most social networking sites are free, easy to join, and simple to set up. Many also make it easy to find people who might be interested in your craft. Once you find them, you simply invite them to be your "friend." Assuming they accept, you are on your way to creating a list of customers and craft associates whom you can keep informed about your next craft show or latest project.

But remember, security on these social networking sites is imperative. If you set up a Facebook page for your followers, I recommend enabling all the security features that keep your private information private.

Needless to say, personal information has no business on a professional Facebook page. Your craft page is not the place to post photos of that wild party you attended last month.

Twitter

Twitter is a real-time information network which spreads small bits of information instantly. The number of characters is limited, so the general idea is to pique interest with some "headlines" and then direct readers to your blog or website. The power of a "tweet" can't be underestimated in this age of instant communication.

With Twitter, you want to find other craft-minded people and connect to them. You sign up and activate your account, fill out your profile, then start searching for craft-related people. Start following them, and many will follow you back. It's that simple.

It's best not to follow just anyone on Twitter, but to concentrate on those with similar interests. The idea is to build a community.

Security

Never forget that information you post online can be mined for criminal purposes. It behooves you to play it safe in cyberspace.

To this end, I would suggest you never post your phone number or street address. If an address is necessary, consider getting a post office box so your physical location is not available.

Sometimes people forget that being online does not mean you're anonymous. Any dirty laundry you choose to post may come back to haunt you, so play it safe and be clean. These days, employers are researching prospective hires for nefarious connections or habits, so under no circumstances should you post compromising photos or information.

Backing Up Your Computer

One little-heralded but critical aspect of using your computer for business (and/or pleasure) is to *back it up* on a regular basis.

The easiest way to do this is to use an external hard drive. These can be purchased at warehouse stores for a reasonable sum. And remember, whatever you spend on a backup system will be well worth it *when* your computer crashes. And most of us know a computer crash is not a matter of "if," it's a matter of "when." Do you really want to lose your precious family photos or critical business information because you did not create a backup?

While daily use files can be backed up on a thumb drive, an external hard drive is needed to handle the large programs and extensive number of photos most people keep archived on their computers.

Make a full-scale backup part of your weekly routine. If you know you'll be gone for a predictable period each week—for church or school or a meeting—then set your computer to back up while you're gone.

Whatever schedule you use, the important thing is to *do it*. Untold personal and professional anguish is caused when a computer crashes, and it's doubly dreadful because it's so preventable.

10 Managing Your Craft Business

Reading and studying are excellent ways to learn about business management, but you can't learn everything you need to know about managing from books, or even from a four-year college program in business administration. You must also learn from experience, which is another reason for starting your home-based craft business on a part-time basis. Moreover, you should possess certain attributes that are even more important than education and experience.

You can manage a business without formal schooling in business management. You can manage a business without prior management experience. You cannot expect to succeed, however, without common sense and the capacity to think and reason. An indecisive person who has trouble solving problems should forget about starting a home-based business.

Identifying Problems

What kinds of problems might the home-based craft professional have to face? Every aspect of your business can be problematic. You can have problems with vendors, customers, and other people. Your business vehicle, craft machinery, and office equipment can give you trouble. You can have financial, legal, and operational difficulties. You can have insurance problems, tax troubles, and minor irritations or major worries over bookkeeping, paper shuffling, phone service, time management, printing, plumbing, electricity, the neighbor's cat, termites, and door-to-door peddlers.

The potential seems boundless, but the right attitude and strategy can keep catastrophes contained. Understand that running a business is mainly a matter of encountering, identifying, and solving problems, big and small. Most of what we've covered so far in this book has to do with managing minor problems and avoiding major ones.

Don't Needlessly Complicate Matters

A problem is any matter, concern, or situation that poses an obstacle or causes some degree of difficulty or perplexity in the carrying out of a task. It's as simple as that. Too many people, however, make too big a deal out of problem solving. If you can think, you can make decisions. If you can make decisions, you can solve problems. If you can solve problems, you can run a successful business.

In recent years I've read a number of reports and articles written by business consultants and other authorities. I have watched some of these experts in action and have grown especially wary of business gurus who turn decision-making and problem-solving processes into complex and convoluted exercises. If I followed all their silly suggestions, I'd never get anything done.

There's also a tendency among business consultants and academics to complicate otherwise simple processes with highfalutin terminology. With the possible exceptions of sociology and literary criticism, no other discipline is more encumbered with buzzwords, catchphrases, jargon, and invented terms.

It's always best to anticipate problems so that you can avoid them or deal with them comfortably and effectively. Like life, however, business is full of surprises. If you're smart, you'll take them in stride and learn from them.

I'm frequently reminded of the old medical joke in which the physician asks the patient what the problem is. The patient raises an arm and says, "It hurts when I do this." The doctor responds, "Then don't do that." How many times have I made some foolish move and instantly regretted it? Pardon me while I count. Invariably, I think to myself or even say aloud, "I won't do that again." Live and learn.

Managing Time

Time management is a matter of knowing everything you have to do and how much time you have to accomplish it, then assigning priorities to most tasks and creating a schedule that allows you to get everything done. Everything. You can't get by with managing only your business time; you must manage all your time to make room for the many jobs, chores, and attendant details in your busy life.

Production Control

If there's a secret to success in any business—large or small, corporate conglomerate or sole proprietorship—it's production control. Any business manager who ignores or fails to understand the importance of production control is headed for disaster.

Of course, every product-oriented business depends to some extent on ideas, designs, and creative thinking. But without careful control of the production processes that ensures timely manufacture and delivery of top-quality products at the lowest possible cost, the creative processes are futile exercises. If creativity is the heart of your business, production control is the central nervous system.

The job of production control comprises five phases or steps:

1. *Analyzing production needs.* Once you have created a workable and salable design, you must determine its manufacturing requirements. What materials will you need to acquire? What tools are required; will you need to buy any? How does production of this product affect the production of other products? Will you be making all the components, or can you buy some ready-made parts?

2. *Planning the production process.* Product parts must be acquired, made, or modified, then put together. What is the proper sequence of acquisition and assembly? How is the product to be finished? Should some parts be painted, varnished, or otherwise finished before assembly? How many different tool setups are required? All of this must fit into a working production plan.

3. *Implementing the production plan.* Make sure essential materials, supplies, and parts are conveniently and safely contained and readily accessible near the production area. Have all required tools nearby. Make sure machinery is set up for the first production phase and, if possible, any subsequent phases. Keep the production plan handy for later tool setups.

4. *Streamlining production.* During initial production, remain alert for operations that can be accomplished more safely, quickly, and efficiently. Watch for any possible production alterations that could save time, money, or both. Set production goals at the outset, and try to exceed them as you proceed. Analyze all operations during and after production and take careful notes on ways to improve any phase. To save on tool setup time, watch for production phases that are compatible with other products in your line.

5. *Conducting micro cost analysis.* Macro cost analysis is important as a way of letting you know how your business is doing overall and how it can be improved. Micro cost analysis of each product and each part of each product will give you a much better picture of where your production strengths and

weaknesses are and where and how you can improve production to reduce costs or make your operations more cost-effective.

For most products, machine setup is the most time-consuming and costly part of production. When coming up with a prototype of any design, I usually spend more time on machine setup and organization than I do on actual assembly and finishing. So as I develop my production plan, I look for opportunities to batch-process and try to implement them wherever possible.

A word of warning is in order, however. Although batch processing of components reduces costly setup time, it can lead to monotony and result in safety hazards, especially when power tools are used. So part of your production plan should include some relief steps that will help alleviate boredom and keep you alert.

Let's say you have 300 identical parts to cut with a table saw, and you know it will take about an hour to complete this step. After about twenty minutes the job's going to get monotonous, and your concentration will waver as your mind drifts. At this point it could be dangerous to continue cutting, but it would be silly to stop after cutting 100 parts and set up for the next cutting step, only to have to return to those remaining 200 parts and retool twice more for them.

It's better to include steps that will relieve monotony while maintaining an efficient production schedule. For example, if the parts you're cutting will need light sanding before assembly, you can spend twenty minutes cutting 100 parts and then move to the sander, where that relief step might take ten minutes. Return to the saw for the next twenty minutes and sand for ten more. One more cycle, and you'll be finished cutting and sanding 300 parts—and will have done so in safety.

Batch finishing—staining, painting, varnishing, stenciling, texturing, weathering, antiquing, and such—also saves time and promotes efficiency. It's also possible to gang-finish quantities of several different products at once.

Improving Production

Although production control is mainly associated with manufacture, it's also inextricably tied to planning and to marketing. There are more ways of improving production than simply increasing output or directly reducing costs. So solving production problems often means examining production plans at one end and marketing strategies at the other.

Streamlining Production

One aspect of increasing the profit margin on your craft is to streamline your production techniques.

This simply means learning to shave anywhere from seconds to minutes off each step of manufacturing. Over time, seconds and minutes can add up to days and months of saved labor. And as any professional knows, *time* is the costliest aspect of making anything. Any manner in which you can save yourself time will increase your productivity.

However, you cannot sacrifice quality in the quest to streamline. If you decide to skip a step in the manufacturing process in order to save time, but then customers start to complain that seams are coming apart or pieces are falling off, then clearly skipping that step compromises your quality. And you don't want to develop a reputation for making shoddy crafts.

Streamlining also means knowing what products or aspects of a product aren't worth your time to do. If a customer thinks your craft could be improved by adding glazed flowers all over it, you need to examine (a) how difficult and time-consuming that extra step would be, and (b) if any *other* customer thinks glazed flowers are an improvement—and is willing to pay extra for the addition. If not, it might be best to stick to your original design.

On the other hand, perhaps the customer is right, and the glazed-flower option becomes one of your best sellers. Examining the cost/benefit ratio in advance may determine whether you give the variation a chance.

Ready-Made Components

Another important part of your production plan is determining whether to make all the necessary parts for any product or buy ready-made components when they're available. Of course, cost is the primary determinant in this decision, but remember, time is money. Even though you might save a good bit by manufacturing any component, you could end up spending more time than the saving justifies.

When I began making mug trees, I showed one to a friend and fellow craftsman. He dutifully admired it and then said, "I didn't know you had a lathe." When I acknowledged that I didn't, he was astonished that I was actually paying good money for ready-made mug-tree pegs when I could turn my own for about half the price.

Well, to make my own pegs, I'd have to invest several hundred dollars in a lathe, which is only a minor deterrent, inasmuch as I could put the tool to good use on other products. Even if I had a lathe, though, I still couldn't make the pegs as cheaply as I can buy them ready to use.

In my early cost analysis for the same project, I looked at the possibility of making another component myself: square felt cushions from $1/4$-inch-wide felt tape. By buying the tape in 900-foot rolls, I could hold my felt costs to about 3 cents per unit. But I would also have to cut four squares per unit, which may not seem like much labor, until you imagine cutting 200 squares for fifty mug trees. I decided to spend a dime a unit for $1/4$-inch felt dots instead.

What's important is that you consider the feasibility and cost efficiency of using ready-made parts wherever you can. Determine what it costs in *cash* and *labor* to make the component yourself and what it costs to buy the finished component.

Handling Growth

There's nothing wrong with modest beginnings. In fact, I'd recommend you start small. But you must plan to succeed, which means you must plan to expand, perhaps several times, and eventually to limit or curtail expansion. In short, you must control the growth of your business.

If you operate your home-based craft business intelligently and aggressively, it will grow—most rapidly during the first few years. You could also experience rapid growth whenever you branch out into another craft area. You must pace that growth according to your abilities, resources, and available space.

Eventually, you will be getting all the business you can handle, at which time you must decide whether to level off or continue expanding. This is not as easy a decision as it might first appear.

Many entrepreneurs equate growth with success and insist that in order to succeed a business must grow, which is true to some extent. It is, indeed, important for a business to grow during its formative years. It can be dangerous, however, to extend the growth notion too far: to think that the faster a business grows, the more successful it will be; or to believe that if a business doesn't continue to grow, it is destined to fail.

It is possible to grow too fast—that is, to take on more than you can handle. If prices quoted to your clients or customers are based on a business run by one person, you can get into serious trouble if you must hire help or farm out work to others to honor your commitments and meet deadlines. Not only might this reduce or even eliminate your profits, but it can also eat into your operating capital. Your dilemma is that you must either break your promises and miss deadlines or spend extra money to get the work done on time. You can't operate that way and expect to stay in business.

Even with proper planning and managed growth, you will eventually reach a saturation point. That's when you'll have to decide whether to level off or hire help.

Working with Others

Sometimes the promise of high profits can cloud one's vision and impair judgment. There's nothing wrong with providing jobs for others, but you must keep in mind why you wanted your own home-based craft business in the first place. Was it to build an empire, or was it to provide yourself with a satisfying career and a comfortable income? In case of the former, you must be willing and able to accept the hassles and responsibilities that come with empire building. If you're among the latter group, you must know how to manage and curtail growth and how to handle potential growth problems.

As your business grows, you will discover that there are times when seven days aren't enough to get the week's work done. A number of factors can contribute to scheduling problems and the need for careful scrutiny of your business's labor requirements.

- *Seasonal aspects.* You might find that there are times of the year when you have more work than you can handle. The holiday season, for example—from October through Christmas Eve—is a time of high-volume sales for most crafts. Mother's Day and Father's Day are other peak times for craft gifts. Where I live, the tourist season is important.
- *Rush orders.* You won't be in business long before you discover that few customers and clients plan ahead. Everybody, it seems, needs it yesterday. Instead of paying attention to inventory and placing timely orders, even clients who should know better will end up phoning you only when they've run out of your products.
- *Special projects.* From time to time you will probably land jobs or be commissioned to do work outside of or in addition to your usual business. Often these can be lucrative projects that you can't afford to turn down. Indeed,

you might pursue or even initiate them yourself. As well as they may pay, they can put additional demands on your business that call for extraordinary measures.

- *Accumulated chores.* Dealing with all the above problems will force you to set priorities and to put off low-priority tasks until time permits you to address them. These lesser jobs can eventually grow into major responsibilities that cry for immediate attention.

When faced with these or similar circumstances, you have several choices. Enlisting the help of a family member could be the simplest solution, but this isn't always possible. In my own business, my wife is a great helpmate. But she has her own full-time career, so she isn't available during the course of a normal workweek.

If you need help with your work and, for one reason or another, no one in your family can come to your aid, you might have to consider hiring help. Your alternatives are to hire personnel on your own or to work with a local employment service.

Often, hiring help only adds to your burdens, so I recommend you do this as a last resort. You'll probably need to advertise. Then you'll have to screen and interview prospective employees. In order to attract competent applicants, you'll have to offer a competitive wage and certain fringe benefits.

State and federal regulations make hiring personnel difficult, expensive, and time-consuming. You must pay for unemployment insurance, Social Security, and workers' compensation. You're responsible for deducting Social Security taxes as well as federal, state, and local income taxes from an employee's pay and submitting the deducted funds to the various agencies with all the appropriate forms.

On top of all that, you'll have to pay for a certain amount of nonproduction: holidays, sick days, personal days, and vacation time. And you will probably be responsible for some kind of health insurance. The paperwork for all this can be a nightmare, and the cost can soar to an amount equivalent to 40 to 45 percent of the employee's pay. In other words, if you pay a full-time employee $10 an hour, or $400 a week, your actual costs will be in the neighborhood of $14.50 an hour, or $580 a week.

After your business's workload subsides or returns to normal, you'll have to lay off anyone you've hired. This can be a depressing duty for you and certainly an unhappy event for the employee. What's more, it can increase premiums for unemployment compensation insurance.

If you hire people to help produce craft items, the IRS will probably consider them employees if they are following procedures you have developed for your products, even if they're not working on your premises.

On the other hand, I know of two woodworkers who regularly hire artists as independent contractors to paint scenes on their woodcraft items. I know cabinet-makers who sometimes hire woodcarvers as independent contractors to carve door and drawer panels. The big difference here is that the artists and carvers are allowed the artistic freedom to paint and carve their own scenes and impressions without following someone else's step-by-step procedures.

The best advice I can offer is to describe in writing how you intend to hire and occupy independent contractors, and allow a local IRS agent to review your plan and advise you. Get the agent's response in writing or get a notation on your plan signed and dated. If local agents are reluctant, you can request an official ruling in writing from the Internal Revenue Service in Washington, D.C.

Hiring Temporary Help

You'll probably be far better off hiring temporary help through an employment service, not to be confused with an employment agency. Both are companies that provide workers for other businesses. The employment service tests, screens, hires, and trains the workers; pays their salaries; provides all their benefits; makes all the necessary payroll deductions; and sees to all the paperwork.

Well before you have an actual need, you should find out what sort of temporary help is available in your locale. Check with the local chamber of commerce or Small Business Development Center. Look in the Yellow Pages or online under such headings as "Employee Leasing," "Employment—Temporary," and "Employment Contractors—Temporary Help."

Most such companies have an employee pool with a wide range of skills in a variety of fields. Most have clerical help and skilled office workers available, and some have people competent in certain specialty areas.

When you use an employment service, you pay an hourly rate to the service, which then pays the employee and keeps a portion for the service. The rate you pay obviously must be higher than what you would pay to an employee you hire yourself but will probably work out to be a better deal for you in the final analysis.

For example, if the employment service charges you $15 an hour for the kind of employee you could have hired directly for $10 an hour, this might seem exorbitant at first glance. Consider, however, that your $10-an-hour employee will actually cost you $14.50 an hour. So in essence, you end up paying a mere 50 cents an hour to avoid all the time-consuming chores and paperwork associated with advertising for, interviewing, screening, training, and paying an employee.

Independent Contractors

An alternative to hiring help is to use the services of an independent contractor—someone who, like you, is self-employed and works by the job or by the hour, under contract. You and the contractor agree in writing to what the job entails and how much you will pay. The contractor is then responsible for doing the work as stipulated, paying self-employment and income taxes, and filing the necessary forms.

If you use independent contractors in your work, there is one form you might have to file. The Internal Revenue Service requires you to file a Form 1099-MISC for any independent contractor you pay more than $600 during the tax year.

You can advertise for an independent contractor in a local newspaper's classified section or online classifieds like Craigslist, or you can try to find someone through other sources. Put the word out at local galleries, gift shops, and stores that sell arts-and-crafts supplies. Other good sources include arts-and-crafts schools, some types of technical schools, and any nearby college or university with an art department, especially one offering courses in applied arts.

You can hire an independent contractor for any job for which you might otherwise hire an employee. The big difference is that you can avoid most of the headaches and nuisances associated with being an employer.

You can also hire independent contractors for jobs you would otherwise do yourself—either in your business or in your home. When you hire a plumber or an electrician, you're hiring an independent contractor, and either the contractor or one of his employees will take care of the job. If you know how to do such work yourself, you can save money. Some contractors, however, might save you money in the long run by freeing you from the task and thereby allowing you to make more money, hour for hour, than you have to pay the contractor. And there may be some jobs you simply don't want to do.

If a light switch or electrical outlet needs replacing, I'm not about to hire an electrician who will charge me $65 (probably much higher elsewhere, especially in big cities) when I can buy the fixture for less than $5 and do the job in five minutes.

On the other hand, if I can hire an independent contractor for jobs I hate doing, for less than I can make during the time the jobs take, hiring the contractor makes good sense. Recently, I had a list of repair and maintenance jobs I gave to an independent contractor. All were tasks I've normally taken care of over the years—such as cleaning eaves, replacing soffit-vent screens, cleaning the roof and skylights, and replacing broken chimney guy wires—but they would have taken me two full weekends, precious free time I didn't want to give up. The handyman I hired did all the jobs in three days and charged me $280, which was far less than I made in those three days.

A warning is in order here, however. Be careful to avoid running afoul of IRS regulations when hiring independent contractors to help in your business. Remember, an independent contractor is self-employed and sells products or services to others. An agent who represents you, sells your work at trade shows or to shops and galleries, and keeps a percentage of the sale price as a commission qualifies as an independent contractor. A computer consultant you hire to help set up a system and perform other services as required is an independent contractor.

Collaborating

Collaboration is another way to get help on jobs without hiring employees. In a collaboration you work with one or more other persons to complete a project. For example, you might work with another artisan or artist on a commission or a specific job. You might also collaborate regularly on an entire line of products.

You can handle such informal partnerships in a number of ways. Where the work of each party is about equal, you can equally split costs and profits. You can hire a collaborator at that person's hourly or daily rate or on a per-piece basis. You can even work out a swap arrangement whereby you and your collaborator swap services and then sell your own products individually.

Professionalism

While crafters are undoubtedly experts in making their particular craft, many fall short of cultivating professionalism in their business activities.

Professionalism includes such things as paying bills on time, keeping promises, meeting deadlines, and fulfilling expectations, many of which become crucial when your business expands and/or you start hiring outside help. It also means dressing, behaving, and speaking in a manner that shows you mean business. It means treating customers and suppliers with respect and courtesy. In other words, don't make it difficult for people to do business with you. Whether you are producing for wholesale or retail, your attitude should be pleasant and approachable.

A professional attitude includes keeping your (non-legitimate) complaints to a minimum. It means not bad-mouthing other vendors or, heaven forbid, craft event coordinators. It means not developing a reputation as a difficult or even unethical crafter.

Crafters whose products are superb but whose attitudes are bad don't get much business—or at least not much repeat business. It's been said that a craft business won't thrive on new business. It needs return business. You'll only get that if you act like a professional.

Professionalism goes beyond attitude and into actions. For example, how tidy and attractive is your booth at a craft fair? Is your website easy to negotiate? Do you take precautions to safeguard customers' financial information?

How about a professional approach to sales? Obviously learning to sell your product is an integral part of your business, yet a surprising number of people don't seem able to talk about their product with enthusiasm, knowledge, or salesmanship. Learn to sell your product through speech. If you can't discuss the merits of your craft with animation and enthusiasm, how can you expect anyone else to listen or agree? Or buy?

Promptness is the mark of a professional; courtesy is the mark of a person who is pleasing to deal with. So in all your communications, be prompt and courteous. See to all business correspondence in a timely fashion and return phone calls within twenty-four hours if possible.

Business Communication

Many small-business operators fail to fully appreciate how important written and oral communications are to every business, regardless of its size, product, or service. From the onset, you must be prepared to handle all communication professionally and to document all aspects of your business.

Letterhead and Business Cards

A large amount of modern communication is done by e-mail these days, rendering the need for costly letterhead and business envelopes largely unnecessary. Business cards are still recommended, however. Consider using such inexpensive online sources as Vistaprint.com for your printing needs.

When you wish to communicate by letter, you can create your own letterhead by incorporating a suitable logo and printing it yourself on high-quality paper. This way you only print the letterhead you need, rather than going through the expense of having a full box of custom-printed sheets made up.

A word of caution about sending e-mails or letters: In this age of texting and other abbreviated communication, spelling and proper grammar have taken a nosedive. There is no substitute for a carefully crafted message and no excuse for bad English, poor spelling, or other signs of sloppiness when you are trying to express yourself as a professional.

If you wish to create a logo for your business, you might want to enlist the aid of a graphic artist to provide original art or work with you to come up with a good design. You'll also find useful information and ideas in the book *How to Design Logos, Symbols and Icons* by Gregory Thomas.

Try to make your logo simple, uncluttered, and attractive. If possible, avoid artwork that might date the design. You will use your logo often and become associated with it. For that reason, you shouldn't change it unless absolutely necessary, and then make as few modifications as possible.

Document Your Transactions

Get into the habit of documenting all your business transactions in some way. This doesn't mean you have to write down everything you do in narrative form, although you sometimes should. Every time you write up a work order or prepare an invoice, you are documenting a transaction, so keep copies for your files. Also make a copy of every business letter you write; it can be a carbon copy, carbonless copy, photocopy, or computer copy.

Don't delete your business e-mails, but instead keep them archived. This way you can locate any e-mails with customers and suppliers for reference. (Use the search feature on your e-mail program to help find older communications.)

What about documenting phone calls? You have several options. If you keep a business diary, you can log your phone calls there. Some businesses maintain phone diaries for documenting all telephone communications. I don't keep a business diary; nor do I keep a phone diary. I keep a planner system to document my day-to-day operations. When I need to take important notes, I use ruled yellow pads I buy by the dozen; then I date the notes and route them to their proper files. I keep one of these pads near each of my telephones so that I can take notes on important conversations. I date and file them as I do other notes.

Why all the documentation? It keeps you from relying on what might prove to be an unreliable memory. It helps you get jobs done the way customers want them done. It provides dated references for any necessary follow-up or other action. It provides additional documentation to support tax write-offs. It also protects you and your business in a variety of ways and can be used as evidence in a court of law.

Follow-Up

Follow-up is essential and should be timely, but don't make it any more complicated than it needs to be. I often hear colleagues talk about keeping follow-up logs for all their projects and correspondence. They list everything they send out, the date sent, destination, and other information they deem essential. I don't do any of that, yet I have a follow-up system that will rival any in efficiency.

Everything in my business has a paperwork connection. My invoices and statements are carbonless two-part forms—original to the customer, copy for my files. When I write a query, proposal, or business letter, I keep a copy in a separate file or tray. The job of follow-up is a simple matter of going to the file or tray at the end of each month and examining the contents for anything that requires attention.

I send statements to any clients who haven't paid their bills that month. I then attach a copy of each statement to any pertinent paperwork, such as work orders and invoice copies, and return it to the Accounts Receivable tray. Any account still unpaid thirty days later gets a late charge added to that month's statement.

I don't have to do a tremendous amount of follow-up. In fact, with my receivables, it's usually a matter of just pulling all the copies of invoices, statements, and such as they're paid. There are usually only a few left at the end of a month, and some months there's nothing left in the tray except that month's new billing.

For those who prefer to use their computers, you can utilize the "tickler" features in some bookkeeping software, which will provide pop-up reminders for any follow-up requirements.

Procrastination

As you can see, I put this section off until last. Despite all the words of warning in the various guides for small-business operators and home-based entrepreneurs, procrastination is not the damning malady we're led to believe. Actually, I think most of us are procrastinators by nature. In fact, I'm not sure I could trust (or believe) anyone who claims never to have procrastinated. The trick is to avoid giving in to the urge too often and never to jeopardize a deadline simply because you didn't feel like doing a job.

Few chronic procrastinators end up running their own businesses. Anyone who's that prone to putting things off is also apt to put off starting a business.

Anyone with brains enough to get up in the morning knows you can't constantly put jobs off and expect your business to succeed. There will be days when you just don't feel like working or doing jobs you hate; I assure you of that. But you'll get the work done anyway, because that's your job, and you're a professional. The success of your business depends on those simple facts.

Should you worry about procrastination? I think you can put that off for now.

Appendix A:
Selected Bibliography

Attard, Janet. *The Home Office and Small Business Answer Book*. 2nd ed. New York: Owl Books, 2000.

Brown, Bruce C. *How to Use the Internet to Advertise, Promote and Market Your Business or Web Site—With Little or No Money*. Ocala, FL: Atlantic Publishing Company, 2006.

Brown, Bruce C. *The Complete Guide to Google Advertising*. Ocala, FL: Atlantic Publishing Company, 2007.

Charmasson, Henri J.A. *Patents, Copyrights, and Trademarks for Dummies*. Indianapolis, IN: Wiley Publishing Inc.; 2nd ed., 2008.

Collier, Marsha. *eBay For Dummies*. Indianapolis, IN: Wiley Publishing Inc.; 6th ed., 2009.

Downing, Douglas, et al. *Dictionary of Computer and Internet Terms*. 10th ed. Hauppage, NY: Barron's, 2009.

Gillin, Paul. *The New Influencers: A Marketer's Guide to the New Social Media*. Sanger CA: Quill Driver Books/Word Dancer Press, 2007.

Gumpert, David E. *How to Really Start Your Own Business*. 4th ed. Needham, MA: Lauson Publishing Co., 2003.

Harper, Stephen C. *The McGraw-Hill Guide to Starting Your Own Business: A Step-by-Step Blueprint for the First-Time Entrepreneur*. 2nd ed. New York: McGraw-Hill, 2003.

Hornung, Clarence P. *Treasury of American Design*. New York: Abradale Press, 1997.

J. K. Lasser Institute. *J. K. Lasser's Your Income Tax Guide*. New York: Prentice-Hall, published annually.

Lewis, Patrice. *The Home Craft Business: How to Make It Survive and Thrive*. eBook, http://patricelewis.com/books.html, 2009.

Meltzer, Steve. *Photographing Arts, Crafts and Collectibles: Take Great Digital Photos for Portfolios, Documentation, or Selling on the Web*. New York: Lark Books, 2007.

Perlman, Corey. *eBoot Camp: Proven Internet Marketing Techniques to Grow Your Business*. Hoboken, NJ: Wiley & Sons, 2008.

Pressman, David. *Patent It Yourself*. 14th ed. Berkeley: Nolo Press, 2009.

Ratliff, Susan. *How to Be a Weekend Entrepreneur: Making Money at Craft Fairs and Trade Shows*. Phoenix: Marketing Methods Press, 1991.

Rose, Grace Berne. *The Illustrated Encyclopedia of Crafts and How to Master Them*. Garden City, NY: Doubleday & Company, 1978.

Silber, Lee. *Self-Promotion for the Creative Person: Get the Word Out About Who You Are and What You Do*. New York: Three Rivers Press, 2001.

Thomas, Gregory. *How to Design Logos, Symbols and Icons: 24 Internationally Renowned Studios Reveal How They Develop Trademarks for Print and New Media*. Palm Coast, FL: How Design Books, 2003.

Zimmerman, Jan. *Web Marketing for Dummies*. Indianapolis, IN: Wiley Publishing Inc.; 2nd edition, 2008.

Appendix B:
Source Directory

Associations

American Craft Council
1224 Marshall Street NE, Suite 200
Minneapolis, MN 55413-1036
Phone: (612) 206-3100 or 800-836-3470
Fax: (612) 355-2330
E-mail: council@craftcouncil.org
Web: www.craftcouncil.org

The Arts & Crafts Society
5015 SE Hawthorne Blvd., Suite C
Portland, OR 97215
Phone: (503) 459-4422
E-mail: info@arts-crafts.com
Web: www.arts-crafts.com

Craft and Hobby Association
319 East 54th Street
Elmwood Park, New Jersey 07407
E-mail: info@craftandhobby.org
Phone: (201) 835-1200
Web: www.craftandhobby.org

National Association for the Self-Employed

P.O. Box 241

Annapolis Junction, MD 20701-0241

Phone: (800) 649-6273 or (800) 232-6273

(Alaska and Hawaii)

Web: www.nase.org

National Craft Association

2012 East Ridge Road, Suite 120

Rochester, NY 14622

Phone: (585) 266-5472 or (800) 715-9594

Fax: (585) 785-3231

Web: www.craftassoc.com

Craft Fair and Show Directories (Online)

Craft Fair Directory

www.craftfairdirectory.com

Craft Fairs and Shows

www.craftfairsandshows.com

The Crafts Fair Online

www.craftsfaironline.com

The Crafts Report Showfinder

www.craftsreport.com/listings/shows-and-fairs/
showfinder.html

Event Lister

www.eventlister.com

Festival Network Online

www.festivalnet.com

Craft Supplies

Craft Catalog

P.O. Box 1069

Reynoldsburg, OH 43068

Phone: (740) 964-6210 or (800) 777-1442

Fax: (740) 964-6212 or (800) 955-5915

E-mail: sales@craftcatalog.com

Web: www.craftcatalog.com

Create for less

6932 SW Macadam Ave., Suite A

Portland, OR 97219

Phone: (866) 333-4463

E-mail: info@createforless.com

Web: www.createforless.com

Earth Guild

33 Haywood Street

Asheville, NC 28801

Phone: (828) 255-7818 or (800) 327-8448

Fax: (828) 255-8593

E-mail: inform@earthguild.com or
catalog@earthguild.com

Web: www.earthguild.com

Factory Direct Craft

315 Conover Drive

Franklin, OH 45005

Phone: (800) 252-5223

Fax: (800) 269-8741

E-mail: info@FactoryDirectCraft.com

Web: www.factorydirectcraft.com

J&R Industries Inc.
P.O. Box 4221
Shawnee Mission, KS 66204
Phone: (913) 362-6667
Fax: (913) 362-7421
E-mail: Kathy@JandRind.com
Web: www.jandrind.com

Jerry's Artarama
P.O. Box 58638J
Raleigh, NC 27658-8638
Phone: (800) 827-8478
Web: www.jerrysartarama.com

Michaels Arts and Crafts
Headquarters: 8000 Bent Branch Dr.
Irving, TX 75063
Phone: (800) 642-4235
Web: www.michaels.com

National Artcraft
300 Campus Drive
Aurora, OH 44202
Phone: (330) 562-3500 or (888) 937-2723
Fax: (330) 562-3507 or (800) 292-4916
E-mail: sales@nationalartcraft.com
Web: www.nationalartcraft.com

Prima Bead
Phone: 800-366-2218
E-mail: customerservice@primabead.com
Web: www.primabead.com

Sunshine Discount Crafts
12335 Sixty-second Street
North Largo, FL 33773
Phone: (727) 538-2878 or (800) 729-2878
Fax: (727) 531-2739
E-mail: sunshinecrafts@hypernetusa.net
Web: www.sunshinecrafts.com

Credit Reporting Agencies

Equifax
P.O. Box 740256
Atlanta, GA 30374
(800) 865-1111
www.equifax.com

Experian
P.O. Box 2014
Allen, TX 75013
(888) 397-3742
www.experian.com

TransUnion
P.O. Box 2000
Springfield, PA 19022
(800) 888-4213
www.transunion.com

Free Website and Blog Builders

Blogger
www.blogger.com

Blogspot
www.blogspot.com

Doodlekit
www.doodlekit.com

Moonfruit
www.moonfruit.com

Weebly
www.weebly.com

Wix
www.wix.com

WordPress
www.wordpress.com

Magazines

American Artist
VNU Business Media
770 Broadway
New York, NY 10003
Phone: (646) 654-5506
Phone: (866) 851-6574
E-mail: mail@myamericanartist.com
Web: www.myamericanartist.com

American Craft Magazine
1224 Marshall Street NE, Suite 200
Minneapolis, MN 55413
Phone: (612) 206-3100
Web: www.americancraftmag.org

The Artist's Magazine
4700 East Galbraith Road
Cincinnati, OH 45236
Phone: (513) 531-2222
Fax: (513) 891-7153
Web: www.artistsnetwork.com

Crafts 'n Things
Amos Craft Publishing
2400 Devon, Suite 375
Des Plaines, IL 60018
Phone: (847) 635-5800
Web: www.craftsnthings.com

The Crafts Report
P.O. Box 5000
N7528 Aanstad Road
Iola, WI 54945-5000
Phone: (715) 445-5000 or (800) 331-0038
Fax: (715) 445-4053
Web: www.craftsreport.com

Entrepreneur
Entrepreneur Media, Inc.
2445 McCabe Way, Suite 400
Irvine, CA 92614
Phone: (949) 261-2325
Web: www.entrepreneur.com
Subscriptions:
P.O. Box 50368
Boulder, CO 80322
Phone: (800) 274-6229
E-mail: subscribe@entrepreneurmag.com

HOMEBusiness Journal
Online Magazine
Web: www.homebusinessjournal.net

Home Business Magazine
20711 Holt Avenue
P.O. Box 807
Lakeville, MN 55044
Phone: (800) 734-7042
Web: www.homebusinessmag.com

Inc.
375 Lexington Avenue
New York, NY 10017
Phone: (212) 389–5300
E-mail: editors@inc.com
Web: www.inc.com
Subscriptions:
P.O. Box 3136
Harlan, IA 51593
Phone: (515) 248-7694
Phone: (800) 234-0999

Online Search Engines

AltaVista
www.altavista.com

Dogpile
www.dogpile.com

Google
www.google.com

Meta Crawler Web Search
www.metacrawler.com

Mother of All Search Engines
www.mamma.com

Monster Crawler
www.monstercrawler.com

Webcrawler
www.webcrawler.com

Yahoo
www.yahoo.com

Trade Show Directories (Online)

Biz Trade Shows
www.biztradeshows.com

Events Eye
www.eventseye.com

Trade Show Handbook
www.tradeshowhandbook.com

Trade Show News Network
www.tsnn.com

Vantage Trade Shows
www.vantagetradeshows.com

U.S. Government

Federal Web Locator
Web: www.lib.auburn.edu/madd/docs/fedloc.html

FedWorld Information Network
Web: www.fedworld.gov

GovSpot
Web: www.govspot.com

Superintendent of Documents
U.S. Government Printing Office
Washington, DC 20402
Phone: (202) 512-0132
Web: www.gpoaccess.gov

U.S. Copyright Office
Library of Congress
101 Independence Avenue, Southeast
Washington, DC 20559
Phone: (202) 707-3000 or (877) 476-0778
Web: www.copyright.gov

U.S. Patent and Trademark Office
Phone: (571) 272-1000
Phone: (800) 786-9199
Web: www.uspto.gov

Index

About The Authors

Kenn Oberrecht acquired management skills by working for six years in the corporate world. He concurrently attended the University of Cincinnati Evening College, and later attended the University of Alaska. While in graduate school, Kenn began framing pictures, designing woodworking projects, and establishing his home-based business in his spare time. He and his wife, Pat, moved to the Oregon coast in 1975, where he has run a diversified full-time home-based business ever since.

His project designs, feature articles, and photographs have appeared in numerous home-and-workshop magazines, including *The American Woodworker, Black & Decker Build It!, Craftsman at Home, Decks & Backyard Projects, The Homeowner, Popular Mechanics,* and *Woodworker, and Workbench.* He is the author of more than thirty books and revised editions—including the *Home Book of Picture Framing,* second edition—and is a director and past president of the National Association of Home and Workshop Writers

Patrice Lewis received her Bachelor's degree in Zoology from U.C. Davis in 1985 and her Master's degree in Environmental Education from Southern Oregon University in 1995. She has worked extensively in agricultural and biological research projects but chose to work closer to home when children arrived. In 1993 she co-founded Don Lewis Designs with her husband, a home woodcraft business specializing in hardwood drinking tankards.

Patrice is a freelance writer specializing in the areas of crafts, home businesses, rural life, agricultural issues, parenting, homeschooling, and sociopolitical commentary. Her articles have appeared in *The Crafts Report Magazine, Countryside, Grit, BackHome Magazine, Backwoods Home Magazine,* and many print and online places. She has written an e-book entitled "The Home Craft Business: How to Make It Survive and Thrive" (www.patricelewis.com/books.html).